T H E
LESBIAN
SEX BOOK

FOR ELIZABETH

THE LESBIAN SEX BOOK

BY WENDY CASTER

ILLUSTRATED BY JULIE MAY

alyson
books

LOS ANGELES • NEW YORK

NOTICE TO READERS

THIS BOOK IS INTENDED AS A REFERENCE VOLUME ONLY. IT IS NOT A MEDICAL MANUAL. THE INFORMATION CONTAINED IN THIS MANUAL WAS WRITTEN TO HELP READERS MAKE INFORMED DECISIONS ABOUT THEIR SEXUAL PRACTICES AND ABOUT HEALTH ISSUES ASSOCIATED WITH SEXUALITY. IT WAS NOT DESIGNED AS A SUBSTITUTE FOR ANY TREATMENT THAT MAY HAVE BEEN PRESCRIBED BY YOUR PERSONAL PHYSICIAN. IF YOU SUSPECT THAT YOU HAVE A MEDICAL PROBLEM, SEE A COMPETENT PHYSICIAN TO DISCUSS YOUR CONCERNS.

MANUFACTURED IN THE UNITED STATES OF AMERICA.
PRINTED ON ACID-FREE PAPER.

THIS TRADE PAPERBACK ORIGINAL IS PUBLISHED BY ALYSON PUBLICATIONS INC.,
P.O. BOX 4371, LOS ANGELES, CALIFORNIA 90078-4371.
DISTRIBUTION IN THE UNITED KINGDOM BY TURNAROUND PUBLISHER SERVICES LTD.,
UNIT 3 OLYMPIA TRADING ESTATE, COBURG ROAD, WOOD GREEN,
LONDON N22 6TZ ENGLAND.

FIRST EDITION: MAY 1993

02 01 00 99   10 9 8 7 6

ISBN 1-55583-211-3

LIBRARY OF CONGRESS CARD-CATALOG NUMBER: 93-71122

ILLUSTRATION MODELS: TINA PORTILLO AND LESA LESSARD.
COVER DESIGN BY B. ZINDA.

CONTENTS

INTRODUCTION

The Lesbian Sex Book was written predominantly for newly out lesbians, as well as for curious women who don't choose to label themselves; however, experienced lesbians will also find much of interest here. From *Afterplay* to *Who's on Top?*, with dozens of stops along the way (including *Happily Ever After, Kinsey Report, Oral Sex,* and *Penetration*), this book offers a detailed journey through the wonderful world of lesbian sex.

Whether you want to learn "what lesbians do in bed" so that you can do it too, or you seek a new technique (or two or three), the alphabetical arrangement will allow you to wander through the breadth of lesbian sexuality or turn directly to your topic of choice. Throughout the book are ideas to tickle your fancy no matter how much experience you have.

The interviews. While much of my research consisted of reading sex books, both lesbian-oriented and mainstream, the most wonderful and useful information came from seven lesbians who consented to be interviewed, in *great* detail, about their sex lives. The women were guaranteed anonymity so that they could be perfectly frank, and they were. Ranging in age from twenty-two to fifty-six, of different ethnic and racial backgrounds, with all sorts of sexual preferences and habits, these women shared a willingness to testify to the importance of sex in their lives — and to give tips on how to "do it." They are quoted at length.

I asked these women only about their experiences with women, so when they talk about "never having done something" or "always having felt," those "nevers" and "always" refer solely to their lesbian experiences.

Once friends and acquaintances discovered I was writing a sex book, they started sharing their favorite techniques with me, so there is an eighth lesbian quoted in the book who is a composite of all the women who giggled and then whispered to me about the wonderful experiences they had had.

What is lesbian sex? What is a lesbian? For the purposes of this book, lesbian sex is any sex that happens between two (or more) women. And a lesbian is any woman who identifies herself as one.

Another question might be *Who are the lesbians?* That question is impossible to answer. Because so many gay women are closeted, there's no way to know what "most" lesbians do or believe or want or need. But, judging from women who are openly gay, lesbians run the gamut from sexually conservative to kinky, and from monogamous to multipartnered. There is no one right way to be a lesbian.

Vocabulary. I've chosen mostly to use the word *lesbian* in this book, because it is accepted by so many women. For variety, I've also occasionally used the term *gay women,* and *dyke* shows up now and again for flavor. I've also used both *lovemaking* and *having sex* and both *lover* and *partner.* None of these word choices is meant to show preference for a particular belief system or way of relating sexually.

I refer to *the lesbian community* throughout the book for writing ease, though *lesbian communities* might be more accurate. In quotations, the speaker's original vocabulary is retained. (See also *Vocabulary.*)

Goals. Perhaps your goal is to have endless spiritual sex with one woman with whom you will spend your whole life. Or maybe you just want to have fun with various partners. This book honors both choices and all the ones in between. Whatever you choose, some lesbians will support you and others will tell you you're wrong. Ignore everyone and do what feels best for you. It's your life.

How to use this book. Any way you want!

Acknowledgments. I thank Sasha Alyson and Karen Barber for giving me the opportunity to write this book; Erika Shatz and all the other women who debated the topic "lesbians and AIDS" with me; my ex-lovers, particularly Karol Lightner, Diana Denoyer, and Eve, for all they taught me; my writing group, for keeping me on my toes; Dany Adams, for introducing me to bonobos and for being a marvelous friend; my sister Holly, for a million reasons; the wonderful people at San Diego's Blue Door Bookstore (particularly Charles Wilmoth) for letting me use their shop as a research facility and for all their support; Jayne Relaford Brown, for being a great writing buddy; all the lesbian activists and artists whose hard work has improved the world; Penny, for keeping me sane; all the friends who have supported my writing; and Liz, for making it possible for me to put aside my other work and focus on this project.

I am particularly grateful to the women who bravely, humorously, and insightfully shared their sex lives with me for this book.

—WENDY CASTER

A

AFTERPLAY. (Sexual play occurring after orgasm or after sex is "over.")

Many people top off a wonderful meal by lingering at the table over a leisurely cup of coffee or tea. Afterplay is the after-dinner drink of sex.

Afterplay includes cuddling, kissing, stroking, and lying on top of one another and sweating together. A major part of afterplay is vocal, whether "I love you" or "you're so hot" or "mmmmmmmmmm."

Often, there's a special intensity to sex play right after orgasm, with the smallest strokes setting off tingly aftershocks. Particularly if you've just had a deeply emotional experience, your walls are down, and you may both feel a whole-bodied and whole-hearted enjoyment of *everything.* Take time to savor it.

On a more pragmatic level, certain forms of stimulation can become annoying after orgasm, particularly in sensitive areas such as the clitoris and nipples. Broader, slower, more diffuse stimulation lends itself perfectly to afterplay.

The time immediately after sex can be frightening for some women as they wonder if they "did it okay" or if their lover still finds them attractive. Some women become sad as sex ends. If you enjoyed yourself, let her know. If you're freaked out, let her know that, too.

Sometimes the best afterplay is simply talking together quietly while holding one another. (See also *Cuddling; Foreplay; Orgasms; Sex; Spoons.)*

AGE DIFFERENCES. When two women of significantly different ages fall in love, conventional wisdom says the relationship won't work. Differences in maturity and attitudes will outweigh love and passion.

But conventional wisdom is often wrong.

Kathy loved being with a woman thirteen years older than she: "I learned more about sex from her than I had in the whole rest of my life." Twenty-seven-year-old Jessica says, "My favorite lovers have been the ones who are older, with stretch marks and round bellies."

On the other hand, 48-year-old Lydia says, "I don't think I'm ever going to seriously date anybody twenty years younger than I am again. More than a generation doesn't work." Rebecca says she didn't feel free to tell her younger lovers when she was too tired to have sex; she also found it hard to fit into their social circles: "When we were with her peers, I felt like a real old lady."

None of the women interviewed for this book had experienced any problems with age differences during sex, except sometimes when the partners' energy levels varied. Only in attempted relationships did problems arise.

However, with good communication and true caring for each other and with the support of friends (all of which improve any relationship), the mixed-age couple has just as much chance at long-term success as any other sort of couple.

AGING. There's bad news and there's good news.

The bad news is that, with age, sexual lubrication often lessens significantly, as does energy. Knees may no longer allow fancy sexual positions. Health problems may occur more frequently.

The good news is that age brings experience in pleasing yourself and a partner. Commercial lubricants are available at drugstores. Nonacrobatic sex can be intensely fulfilling. And while ageism does exist in the lesbian community, as in all communities, older and old women are often considered attractive sexual and romantic partners by women their own ages, younger, and older.

Nevertheless, the women forty and older interviewed for this book had little positive to say about aging. While they were glad to have commercial lubricants, they missed their own. And while they appreciated maturing emotionally, they disliked the extra weight they put on as well as the loss of skin tone and energy they suffered. It's clear that many women experience the changes of aging unenthusiastically.

But the older interviewees are all still having great sex! At forty-eight, Lydia maintains an active love life with a number of partners. Rebecca, fifty-six, says, "It suits me to have sex where the feeling is very intense but the activity level is low. I'm having possibly the most sexual relationship I've had in ten or fifteen years."

Forty-year-old Suzanne sums up the dichotomy around aging: "There are times I just don't have the energy to have more orgasms. I know I *could*, but do I want to risk cramp and death? On the other hand, I have tremendously more appreciation and enjoyment and finesse. I've learned a lot about my body, and I have confidence too. I can ask for what I want. All the things I've learned in life help in sex, and they more than compensate for not being able to roll in the hay all night." (See also *Age Differences; Menopause.*)

AIDS. Any mention of the topic "lesbians and AIDS" causes sparks to fly in the lesbian and gay community. Our different opinions mix science, politics, anger, paranoia, fear, hope, and denial until anyone listening to this debate may consider replacing her sex life with a commitment to cross-stitching.

The spectrum of opinion is anchored by two schools of thought. The first argues that lesbians are *definitely* at risk for HIV infection through oral sex and digital penetration, but that the male-run medical establishment cares little about women, particularly lesbians, and has refused to devote resources to assessing our risk factors. This point of view is based on the fact that the majority of U.S. large-scale government-backed studies focus exclusively on men.

The second group argues that there is little or no risk of woman-to-woman HIV transmission. This school of thought claims that gay women all too easily believe that we must practice safer sex because lesbians are scared of sex, secretly find our genitals dirty, envy all the attention gay men are getting, and suffer from survivor guilt. Many lesbians (many people!) do indeed fear sex and feel bad about their genitals, and many lesbians do indeed suffer from survivor guilt.

Unfortunately, neither of these belief systems brings us any closer to understanding the biological realities of possible woman-to-woman HIV transmission.

Most lesbians don't know what to think. They believe that cunnilingus transmits HIV sometimes, or only during menstruation, or hardly at all. There are also women who insist that safer lesbian sex is necessary — but just don't practice it.

In the past, Kathy has had sex with two female AIDS educators. One of them mentioned that she utilizes condoms on her dildo to keep from spreading vaginal infections among her many partners, but neither woman asked Kathy about her sexual history or suggested practicing safer sex. The article "Risky Business: Should Lesbians Practice Safer Sex?" (Out/Look) also found that lesbian health educators talk about safer sex considerably more often than they practice it.

In digging through these contradictions, it's important to start with a simple fact: lesbians do get AIDS — but generally not from having sex with other lesbians. Behaviors, not membership in a particular group, cause transmission of HIV. A gay male virgin is at no risk of sexual HIV transmission, while a lesbian who shoots up intravenous drugs or sleeps with men is at high risk. And, yes, some lesbians do sleep with men.

No matter what their sexual identity or gender, all people can become infected with HIV through blood transfusions, sharing needles, or unprotected penetration with a penis.

However, the transmission of HIV through oral sex and digital penetration is believed to be highly inefficient (albeit not impossible). In the article "No Evidence for Female-to-Female HIV Transmission among 960,000 Female Blood Donors" (Journal of Acquired Immune Deficiency Syndromes), the authors conclude, "Despite a potential risk of female-to-female HIV transmission, HIV transmission by this route is probably very uncommon. Public health prevention measures for reducing HIV spread to and among lesbian and bisexual women should focus on the roles of IV drug use and heterosexual contact." And the Terrence Higgins Trust, an AIDS agency in London, has published a poster announcing that oral sex is a *very* low-risk activity and exhorting lesbians to "ditch those dental dams."

However, according to the pamphlet "Lesbians and AIDS: What's the Connection?" that was put out by the Women's AIDS Network of the San Francisco AIDS Foundation, "lesbians who have had sexual contact with people of either sex whose sexual histories are unknown ... may be at risk."

When I called my local blood bank to see if they considered woman-to-woman sex a high-risk activity, I was transferred to half a dozen people and cut off twice before a nurse rudely blurted, "Of course." I asked on what evidence she based this conclusion. She said, "Call the AIDS Project," and hung up.

I did.

I spoke to a male AIDS educator, who also said, "Of course lesbian sex is high risk!" When I asked where he got his information, he said, "*Everyone* knows lesbian sex is a high-risk activity." I asked him who "everyone" was, and he said, "There are publications." I asked which publications, and he said he didn't know exactly. When I insisted on more information, he started talking about "menstrual blood caught in incisions on labia." He was clearly uncomfortable talking about lesbian sex and couldn't pronounce many of the words he used. More importantly, he made no sense, unless lesbians who never bathe often cut their labia and then rub them together like two kids becoming "blood sisters."

In short, finding concrete information on woman-to-woman transmission of HIV — or, more specifically, on transmission through cunnilingus and digital sex — is far from easy. But there are some facts.

Fact 1: *HIV has been found in vaginal secretions and menstrual blood.* The amounts of HIV in these fluids may be sufficient to be infectious under certain circumstances — for instance, if a woman was penetrated by a dildo that retained infected vaginal secretions or menstrual blood.

Fact 2: *Some lesbians are HIV+,* although all of them are believed to have had other risk factors, including sexual experiences with men, histories of IV drug abuse, and blood transfusions.

Unfortunately, the usefulness of these facts in assessing risk has been mitigated by recent developments: some scientists now insist that HIV isn't the cause (or sole cause) of AIDS. With so much controversy surrounding such an important issue, it is imperative that each lesbian decide how she wants to take care of herself sexually.

How some lesbians deal with HIV transmission. The women interviewed for this book have varied beliefs and experiences around woman-to-woman HIV transmission.

Lydia practices safer sex because she believes that no one really knows all the ways HIV is transmitted. Gail's lover insists that they practice safer sex, although Gail believes it is unnecessary to do so. Jessica refuses to perform oral sex on a woman who has not had an HIV antibody test with a negative result; she explains, "I already have an immune system disorder and the last thing I want to do is get AIDS." Rebecca, who also has health problems, follows a similar route: "I worry about HIV a lot. For a while I wouldn't sleep with anyone until we had an AIDS test. Now it's no oral sex until we've had an AIDS test."

Suzanne is monogamous, but when asked if she'd practice safer sex if she were playing the field, she said, "I'd be cautious about who I'd get involved with. I don't think I'd be using dental dams or latex squares or anything like that. But I would not feel comfortable just fucking around — not so much because of HIV but because of other STDs. I think I would probably use rubbers on toys and stuff like that."

Kathy, also in a relationship, says, "On one hand, my mother told me never to put anything into my mouth unless I knew where it had been. On the other hand, I don't want to lick a woman through a piece of latex unless I have a damned good reason."

Assessing risk. To stay safe, keep up to date with new information about AIDS and its transmission, and don't rely only on the mainstream press or only on the gay press, both of which have their limitations and prejudices. Read articles in detail; when "woman-to-woman transmission" is discussed, does it include cunnilingus only? Digital sex? Anal penetration? (If you are into S/M practices that draw blood, it doesn't matter if you're both women; allowing someone else's blood to get into your body is a high-risk activity.)

When evaluating risks, be sure to consider the psychology of AIDS — and of sex. AIDS is a terrifying disease, and some women would rather practice safer sex for the rest of their lives than take even a one-in-a-billion chance of infection. Most lesbians are probably more at risk of dying in a car accident than of getting AIDS from lesbian sex, yet women who would never give up driving are giving up cunnilingus.

This is where the "cooties factor" comes in. In this sex-phobic, genital-phobic, oral-sex-phobic world, fears around cunnilingus may feel familiar and right. In addition, society's antisex atmosphere judges risks taken for sexual pleasure as wanton and sleazy — even though risks taken to win triathlons, to scale mountains, or to succeed in business are seen as heroic and admirable. It's an odd double standard — and an important one to keep in mind when deciding whether to practice safer sex.

If you do believe in female-to-female HIV transmission, don't find excuses not to practice safer sex. Even the most clean and beautiful and aggressively dyky lesbian may have a history of sleeping with men, doing drugs, or prostitution. And if you don't believe in female-to-female HIV transmission, you may still want to follow some safer sex practices to stop or limit the transmission of herpes, yeast infections, and other STDs. (See also *Safer Sex.*)

ALCOHOL AND DRUG USE. A beer or two or a joint every once in a while provides instant relaxation, lowers inhibitions, and eases the way into sex. If you can keep your alcohol and drug use at a casual level, enjoy!

But remember that lowered inhibitions lead to more risk-taking and less body awareness. Avoid drugs and alcohol when practicing S/M, when having sex with someone you don't know, and when practicing safer sex — in other words, at times when you must have your wits about you. And, of course, *never* drive drunk or stoned.

If you find yourself unable to have sex without a drink first, if you miss days at work because of hangovers, if you drive while stoned, if you steal to buy drugs, if you have blackouts, or if you have to drink or do drugs every day, you have a problem. You aren't alone; an estimated 30 percent of lesbians and gay men abuse drugs and alcohol. (This rate is approximately three times the percentage of heterosexual alcoholics and drug abusers, probably because growing up in a homophobic society leaves many lesbians and gay men with lowered self-esteem; also, much lesbian and gay socializing occurs in bars.)

But help is available. Many alcoholics and drug addicts have found sobriety and peace through various 12-step programs, Alcoholics Anonymous being the most famous. As Kathy puts it, "AA saved my life." And so many lesbians are in recovery that Lydia says, "I really like to have sex using cocaine or with a glass of champagne. But these days, a lot of people I meet are in recovery — or they just don't do that. It's a part of my sex life I don't get into much anymore."

Not everyone trusts and approves of 12-step programs. Some people claim that AA's precepts urge alcoholics and addicts to give up their autonomy and turn into useless zombies. This misinterpretation emphasizes the first step ("We admitted we were powerless over alcohol") and ignores the others, which focus on taking responsibility for one's life and becoming a contributing member of society. Anyone who believes that recovering alcoholics and drug addicts are zombies has never actually sat through an AA meeting!

Critics also complain about AA's focus on "God stuff." AA does suggest reliance on a higher power ("as we understand Him"); atheists, agnostics, and people who practice non-Christian religions may indeed find much of AA difficult to swallow. One option is to try Secular Organizations for Sobriety, also known as Save Our Selves; check your phone book to see if there's a local chapter. Another is to sample various AA meetings until you find one at which you're comfortable; the emphasis on "God stuff" varies from meeting to meeting.

For the lesbian alcoholic or drug addict, there is the additional problem of homophobia, which exists in many meetings. You can stay in the closet, but that choice is particularly unattractive in AA, since 12-step groups stress honesty. However, if you come out, other alcoholics may insist that your lesbianism is a symptom of your addiction! They may even suggest that you go to Homosexuals Anonymous to "recover" from your homosexuality. Note, however, that these homophobes do not speak for all of AA; they are just individual bigots. If they get too obnoxious, find another meeting.

Whatever sort of meeting you end up at, whatever its weaknesses and strengths, remember one of the less-publicized AA adages: "Take what helps you and leave the rest."

Call your doctor for more information, or call Alcoholics Anonymous directly; the number's in the phone book. Ask if there are any meetings in your area particularly aimed at lesbians or gays. Lesbian and gay newspapers, hotlines, and community centers can also point you to friendly AA groups.

It may be embarrassing to call AA or go to a meeting, but getting clean and sober will save your life.

Alanon. Since so many lesbians are alcoholics and drug addicts, the odds of you dating, sleeping with, or befriending someone with an abuse problem are high. If you already care a great deal about someone who abuses drugs or alcohol, you too may want to seek support. Alanon is the 12-step group for the loved ones of alcoholics; check your doctor, phone book, or lesbian and gay newspaper, hotline, or center for more information. (See also *Drugs; Safety; Sober Sex.*)

ANAL SEX. Anal sex includes anilingus (licking the anus) and anal penetration. Not all lesbians practice anal sex, but many who do adore it. A friend of Gail's told her, "If you don't enjoy anal sex, it's not being done right!" That statement isn't totally true — after all, there are always individual preferences and variations — but it certainly suggests how exciting anal sex can be.

Penetration. Anal penetration can be done with a finger or fingers or a butt plug or dildo. Butt plugs come in smaller sizes than dildos; they are often made of stiffer material; and they are shaped to stay in the anus comfortably and safely without getting lost in there.

Because of social taboos about the anus, you may fear penetrating someone there, particularly with your fingers, but the anus is a warm and friendly place and nothing to be scared of. Most fears center around feces; however, fecal matter generally hangs out further up the anus than you will penetrate. If you do bump into some, just wash your hands thoroughly afterward. Or wear a latex glove for digital penetration.

When penetrating your partner anally, start by massaging and stroking or licking her anus. Particularly if she has not done this before, gently penetrate her with one very lubricated finger, just a little bit at a time. (Make sure in advance that your nails are trimmed short and smooth, or wear a latex glove.) When you have your finger a little way inside her, stay still so that she can get used to the sensation. You may find that her anus practically sucks you further in; if so, follow her lead. If not, move your finger gently out a bit, then in a little more.

Little by little, you can slip your whole finger in, but don't force it, and make sure she's comfortable every step of the way. If you're not sure that she's enjoying the sensation, ask her. Some women simply don't like anal penetration, and many find it frightening, particularly at first. Over time, she may decide she wants more fingers inside her or she may want to experience a larger butt plug — or she may never want to try anal sex again.

If the woman you are penetrating has experience with this, follow her lead. Perhaps she can talk you through the first time, step by step. Don't worry that her instructions will make sex sound like a classroom; with a bit of playfulness and a bit of attitude, guidance can make the experience *more* sexy rather than less.

If you have never been penetrated anally, explore yourself before you try it with a partner. Put a finger or two inside your anus and explore its internal contours. Remember to use plenty of lubrication. The more you learn about what you like, the more you can guide your eventual partner. (Note: If you have a history of hemorrhoids, you may want to skip anal penetration altogether.)

When being penetrated anally by someone for the first time, make sure you really trust her, physically and emotionally. The anus is one of those "off-limits" places that can bring up surprising emotional responses, and the sensation may feel psychically as well as physically deep.

Have your partner penetrate you with only a finger or two even if you know you have a larger capacity. She needs to learn the contours of your insides, and you're likely to be more tense and less elastic with someone else than with yourself.

As her finger is going into you, you may feel nervous, and it's not unusual to feel as though you need to move your bowels. Relax. Breathe deeply. If you prefer, ask her to stay still or pull out — or to go in deeper! Listen to your body and trust it; all of your preferences are fine, whether they lean toward dismissing anal sex entirely or moving on to gigantic butt plugs.

Fingers that have been in the anus must be washed thoroughly with soap and water before going anywhere else. Penetrating an anus and then a vagina without washing in between practically guarantees infection.

If possible, don't use the same sex toy for anal and vaginal penetration. However, if a dildo or plug is going to be used by more than one partner or in more than one orifice, use a separate condom each time *and* wash the dildo thoroughly between uses to avoid infection.

Anilingus. Anilingus is pretty straightforward; simply lick her anus or put the tip of your tongue into it. This can follow licking her all over her body or massaging her butt, or any other sort of sex play. Many women find having their anus licked to be exquisite, while others are too grossed out to even consider it.

Anilingus, although considered unlikely to transmit HIV, can transmit intestinal parasites and hepatitis. Since viruses and bacteria that were picked up nonsexually can be transmitted via anilingus, doing this practice without a latex barrier cannot be guaranteed safe, even with a monogamous partner. A dental dam provides a fair amount of safety, but be careful to keep track of which side has been touching the anus. If you lose track, *get a new dental dam.* (See also *Communication; Dildos and Butt Plugs; Oral Sex; Penetration; Safer Sex; Sexually Transmitted Diseases.*)

ANATOMY. It is not necessary to have a detailed knowledge of female anatomy to be a good lover, but it doesn't hurt, either. (Please refer to the accompanying illustrations while reading this section.)

First, some vocabulary. The name of the visible female genitals as a whole is the *vulva.* The vulva includes the hairy outer lips and the smooth, hairless inner lips, which are also know together as the *labia.* (Technically, the outer lips are the *labia majora* and the inner lips are the *labia minora.*) Toward the top of the vulva (that is, toward your belly), where the inner lips meet, is a bump known as the clitoris. Stimulating this wonderful nerve-filled organ provides great pleasure, often resulting in orgasm. Moving down from the clitoris, toward your butt, there is an almost invisible hole, which may appear more as a dent in the skin. This is the opening to the urethra, the tube you pee through. Below that is the opening to the vagina. The area between the vagina and the anus is called the *perineum.*

If you look between your legs with a mirror, you first see the hairy outer labia. In many women, the inner labia are also visible, peeking between the outer lips. Open the outer and inner labia to view the clitoris, urethra, and vagina. The flesh of your vulva may be pink or red or purplish or brown, or a combination of shades. Kathy remembers, "One of my ex-lovers had a twat that looked like a sunset!"

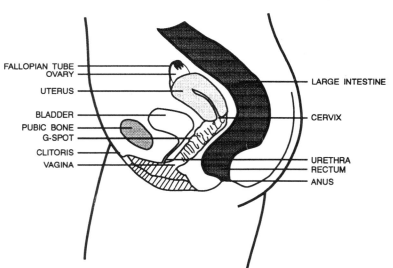

FALLOPIAN TUBE
OVARY
UTERUS
BLADDER
PUBIC BONE
G-SPOT
CLITORIS
VAGINA

LARGE INTESTINE
CERVIX
URETHRA
RECTUM
ANUS

Inside the vagina, under the urethra and in front of the uterus, is the "urethral" or "paraurethral sponge." This sponge is the site of the G-spot and the source of ejaculate for those women who do ejaculate. It also protects the urethra from being injured by vigorous vaginal activity.

If you put your fingers in your vagina and hook them around your pubic bone, so that you're pointing toward the middle of your pubic hair, you are in the area of this sponge. Feel around, and when you reach a particularly sensitive locality, perhaps with a slightly different texture than the rest of the vagina, you have found your G-spot. Touching it may make you feel that you have to pee.

Sometimes, due to the size of your fingers and hands and the length of your vagina, you may not be able to find your own G-spot. Ask a sex partner to help you explore, or try a G-spot attachment on your vibrator.

Every part of the genitals is more or less sensitive, depending on a woman's particular tastes. For instance, some lesbians adore having their labia touched and licked, while others find such stimulation unexciting. Experiment with yourself and your partner to see what feels good, what feels spectacular, and what is just ho-hum.

The internal female organs may also be sites of sexual pleasure. Kathy's lover adores having the general area of her ovaries rubbed, and Suzanne likes pressure at the base of her belly during penetration, for a sort of sexual organ massage. While some women hate having their cervix and uterus bumped during penetration, others love the feeling. Explore these areas carefully, and you're sure to find some hidden treasures.

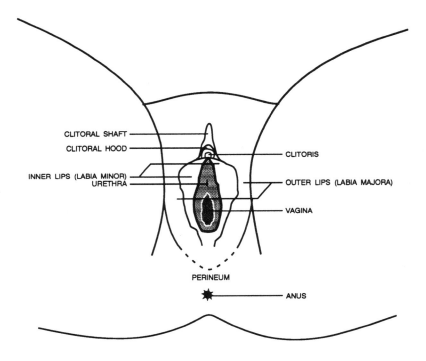

It's fun and informative to examine another woman's genitals and compare them with your own. Although the general layout is the same, there are variations in labia size, clitoris size, coloration, and amount of hair. This is a good time to discuss what sexual stimulation feels good and what doesn't, and the examination may help both partners grow more comfortable with themselves sexually. (See also *Bodies; Clitoris; G-Spot.*)

ANILINGUS. See *Anal Sex* and *Safer Sex.*

ANONYMOUS SEX. See *Casual Sex.*

APHRODISIACS. (Foods, drugs, or other items that enhance sexual pleasure; named after the Greek goddess of love and beauty, *Aphrodite.*)

Throughout history, substances ranging from oysters to cocaine have been rumored to magically stimulate the human libido. Unfortunately, the true sexual effects of these items are nonexistent at worst and transient or dangerous at best.

However, an aphrodisiac is *anything* that enhances sexual pleasure, and a real stimulant doesn't have to be exotic, expensive, or dangerous. Forget Spanish fly and kava kava and try candlelight or a lovely meal instead. Send her sexy notes. Try making love semiclothed, or play out a fantasy. Buy a new sex toy. Watch an erotic video. Do the dishes when it's her turn to do them. (See also *Long-Term Relationships; Romance.*)

APPEARANCES. While mainstream culture glorifies starved-thin young women, lesbians appreciate big women, small women, muscular women, heavy women, wrinkled women, and gray-haired women. The lesbian community also appreciates a larger variety of clothing styles than does the mainstream. Lesbians wear business suits or leather, jeans or dresses, tuxedoes or gowns, shoulder-length curls or mohawks — sometimes in surprising combinations!

While clothing often defines certain lesbian subcultures, with Queer Nationals leaning more to leather and jeans and Career Women donning business suits, few lesbians travel in only one well-defined circle. How the Queer National dresses at work and what the Career Woman slips on for weekend wear may be surprising. And all assumptions shatter when the Queer National and the Career Woman turn out to be the same person!

Of course, not all lesbians appreciate all women, and classism, ageism, racism, fattism, and other -isms do rear their ugly heads in lesbian-land. But compared with mainstream rules of attractiveness, the lesbian community overflows with sartorial freedom.

For many lesbians, attractiveness depends not on clothing or body size or facial prettiness but, rather, on how a woman relates to herself and her sexuality. Not one of the lesbians interviewed for this book mentioned a particular body size or type of looks when describing what she found attractive, though a few did specify preferring butches or femmes.

Jessica explains, "The most incredible turn-on for me is somebody who has what others might not consider to be the perfect body, but she's sexy and she knows it." Gail insists only that a woman take care of herself: "She could be a hundred pounds or three hundred pounds as long as she is well groomed." Lydia sums up her preferences with, "It's more attitude than anything else."

Sometimes lesbians see through different eyes than the rest of the world. Jessica, with her quarter-inch-high flat-top haircut, is often mistaken for a man. However, she says, "I've had lovers tell me, 'Oh you're so feminine, you're so pretty' — and I think, oh, I wish my mother could hear you say that."

A list of lesbian icons neatly reveals the length and breadth of lesbian tastes. Martina Navratilova. Tina Turner. Georgia O'Keeffe. Kitty Tsui. Madonna. k.d. lang. Susan Sarandon.

So, if you're new to the lesbian community, enjoy your freedom! Take time to discover what clothing or costuming you prefer. Explore your trashy side and your conservative side. Clothing won't make you sexy, but your comfort and confidence in how you dress will. (See also *Types.)*

ARGUING. When lovers argue, their emotions explode, anger and fear pulsate, and adrenaline pumps. Then, as the yelling tapers off and the lovers make up, relief replaces fear of abandonment, and passionate arguing easily segues into passionate lovemaking. What a hot way to reconcile! No wonder the sizzling intensity of sex after fighting is legendary. Some people don't even bother to make up; they go directly from arguing to having sex.

But if you find that you and your partner never have sex without fighting first, it's time to explore the tensions between you more deeply. A good, quiet, loving conversation can clear the air, or the support and input of a therapist may be in order.

Ultimately, your comfort with "arguing as foreplay" depends on what you want from a relationship. Kathy stayed with a partner for a year even though they did little but fight, make love, and play video games. She doesn't regret this relationship at all, explaining, "A year of good sex is nothing to sneeze at." But if you want a long-term commitment with growing compatibility and connection, relying on arguments to fuel sex will not take you where you want to go. (See also *Battered and Battering Lesbians.)*

ARMPITS. Shaven or unshaven, armpits are sexy. They are sensitive and soft, and their location suggests other hidden places (Kathy's lover calls them "little crotches"). But deodorant is not sexy. It tastes terrible. Take a shower immediately before sex, or warn your lover that you're wearing deodorant if she's kissing you anywhere near your armpits. (See also *Shaving.*)

ATMOSPHERE. While the old standbys of fireplaces and candlelight dinners rarely fail to set the mood, the ingredients that create the ideal sexy atmosphere vary from woman to woman.

Jenn says, "I love fishnets, and skirts, and high heels. And candles. Probably you should put a bag of chips there too. As soon as I start sex, I get hungry."

Rebecca's ideal sexy scene blends her own preferences with a traditional background: "I was brought up on the movies of the forties, and to me a sexy scene is candlelight and music. And talking — feeling a connection, a bond, through words. And maybe there's dancing and a moon."

Jessica's idea of an erotic scene depends on who's in it, rather than where it occurs: "I like the idea of a really butch woman with a man's shirt on, or a t-shirt and jeans, maybe boots. She would just push me down onto the bed, hold me down, and rip my clothes off — and say nice things to me. I also think dildos and dildo harnesses are an incredible turn-on."

For Gail, "There are those usual places, like a cabin in Lake Tahoe when it's snowing. Also, the woman I'm sleeping with said she's going to strip for me and dance, and I think that's an incredibly sexy thing to do."

Suzanne says, "I have a sexual fantasy with a bed out in the woods, with golden light filtering down through the trees. There are bedside tables with wonderful food — wine and really good fruit — and wooden bedposts and all white white white soft soft soft downy type things on the bed. And a breeze. My other idea of a sexy scene is a harder-edged one, like a bar atmosphere. In reality, it's always too noisy and too smoky, but that sort of lights-down, dance-floor, come-on energy *is* sexy."

A change as small as making love in the living room rather than in the bedroom provides a new atmosphere. Hotels, away from interruptions, responsibilities, and having to do your own dishes, may ignite a fresh sexual spark. But even your same old bedroom, in need of a good dusting, can be transformed by candles and a flower or two.

As you get to know your partner better, setting up the perfect romantic atmosphere for her can become an art form. Surround her with her favorite music, colors, scents, and textures. Wear her favorite clothing. Whether you aim for good sex tonight or romance forever, paying attention to her is the single sexiest thing you can do.

B

BACKRUBS. See *Massage.*

BACKS. Backs are filled with sensual and sexual potential. The curve of a woman's shoulder blades, along her spine, and down to the small of her back, is one of nature's perfect creations. Caress her gently with the palm of your hand, or run one finger along the lines delineated by her bones and muscles. Then stroke her more firmly, almost as if massaging her. Or run your tongue along her spine. Or nibble and bite her all over.

Listen to her responses with your ears and with your fingers. Note what she likes a lot and what she doesn't like as well. And if you're not sure, ask.

BARS. Lesbian socializing once centered around the bars; in some regions, it still does. However, now that many locations offer support groups, sports teams, religious organizations, political events, and social groups, the bars are no longer the be-all and end-all of the lesbian community. But many of us still enjoy them.

Bars offer dancing and variety and excitement. They're good places to find friends and lovers, and some women go to bars simply to be surrounded by lesbians.

Women interested in casual sex often find overnight lovers at bars. Meeting partners this way requires caution; drunk women are not safe or great lovers, and should you become seriously interested (it does happen), you may find that she has a drinking problem. But there's an honesty and openness to meeting a lover-for-the-night at a bar; it's okay to be blatant and straightforward, and if one woman says no, there are always others to ask.

Of course, not all meetings at bars lead to sex that night, nor do all women who go to bars drink. Many sober women in 12-step programs continue to socialize at bars, simply switching from beers to club sodas.

In a city with many women's bars, take the time to find the one where you feel most comfortable. Some bars cater to hard drinkers, others to hard dancers. The clientele at one place will wear tomorrow's "in" clothing, while at another bar the women dress casually, for comfort. Some bars are hangouts for playing pool, and others are 100 percent pickup joints. The names can be a clue; if you are a sexually

conservative woman looking for a quiet conversation with a like-minded woman, the Clit Club is probably not for you.

Many bars offer dance lessons, including two-step, country and western, and even ballroom dancing. These lessons provide a graceful way to meet other people while having fun.

BATHTUBS. See *Water*.

BATTERED AND BATTERING LESBIANS. What exactly is battering? In *Naming the Violence: Speaking Out about Lesbian Battering* (edited by Kerry Lobel), Barbara Hart explains that battering can be physical, sexual, verbal, economic, psychological, or homophobic. Along with punching, biting, and assaults with weapons, battering can include rape, slashing car tires or clothing, humiliation, and insults. If your partner threatens to tell your family or boss that you're a lesbian, that's battering. If your partner forces you to have sex with other people, that's battering. Fits of anger, sleep interference, and lying are all forms of battering.

Yes, lesbians do abuse other lesbians. It's not a popular fact, and many women choose to deny it. Battering is dismissed as "something that men do," and the lesbian who suggests otherwise may be seen as a traitor. Many women refuse to acknowledge that *any* woman can be violent. But keeping our heads in the clouds does nothing to help the battered woman or the batterer. To confront a threat as real and as dangerous as abuse, honesty is imperative.

The step after acknowledging that such abuse occurs is acknowledging that there is no excuse for it. However, according to *Violent Betrayal: Partner Abuse in Lesbian Relationships,* by Claire M. Renzetti, lesbians are more likely than straight women to stay in abusive relationships, justifying the abuse as being "societally induced."

The battered lesbian who does leave an abusive relationship often suffers double oppression. She may receive little support from the lesbian community, particularly if the woman who battered her is popular in that community. In addition, she may find herself unwelcome at shelters and therapy groups aimed at battered (heterosexual) women.

But the situation is improving. Lesbian survivors are starting their own support groups and, in some cases, getting major funding. For instance, Seattle has the government-funded Advocates for Abused and Battered Lesbians; Minnesota has Lesbian Advocacy and Lesbian Battering Intervention; San Diego has the Battered Women Support Group.

If you're in an abusive relationship, you may need help to get out. Call your local lesbian and gay hotline or a social service agency for a support group in your area. If they cannot help you, call a local therapist or a women's center. Also check the phone book and the listings in your local lesbian and gay paper; look under "lesbian," "battering," "abuse," "advocates," and "hotline." Doing this research can be maddening, and you may be referred from person to person or have to listen to long messages that end with still another number to call. However frustrating and frightening the process may be, *stick to it;* you deserve help. Whether with the assistance of friends and agencies, or on your own, you must get away from the batterer.

The bottom line on battery is simple. If your lover abuses you, get away from her and get help. You do not deserve that treatment. And if you batter your lover, *stop it* and get help. It is not acceptable behavior. There is no excuse. (See also *Therapy.)*

BEDS. To enhance your sex life, don't have fights in bed; don't do therapy in bed; and don't dwell on the mundane details of life in bed. Dedicate your bed to sex, cuddling, loving conversation, and sleeping, and it will grow to be a sacred and comfy place, free of any negative associations.

BISEXUALITY. Sex researcher Alfred C. Kinsey believed that all humans could enjoy stimulation from women, men, and themselves. But our linear, strictly bipolar society views people as either heterosexual ("normal") or homosexual ("abnormal"). To survive the bigotry of mainstream society, lesbians and gay men have banded together across the great divide from "normal."

With heterosexuals in one group and homosexuals in another, bisexuals have ended up stuck in the middle. Bigoted straights consider bisexuals to be promiscuous and perverted, and bigoted gays consider bisexuals to be gays too scared to come out — or visitors from the straight world, slumming for kicks. Some lesbians particularly dislike bisexual women, considering them to be male-identified and the source of sexually transmitted disease in the lesbian community.

If you're bisexual, you'll have to deal with these factors, along with your confusion if you're just discovering your sexual preference, plus your anger at not being taken seriously for who you are. It's a tough situation, made even worse because the gay people oppressing you are oppressed themselves, so you'd think they'd know better.

But don't give up your own identity. There are people, female and male, gay and straight, who will accept and love you exactly as you are — and you deserve nothing less. Since more and more bisexuals are coming out, forming their own groups and insisting on inclusion in pre-existing lesbian and gay groups, you will not be alone. Bisexuality is still an unpopular orientation in many communities, but it is no longer a totally isolated one.

BITING. See *Nibbling.*

BLINDFOLDS. See *Bondage.*

BODIES. During sex, we often focus exclusively on the "official" erogenous zones, as though the areas besides vulva and breasts comprise vast desert wastelands. Yet the body is filled with sensitive places.

Rebecca adores thighs: "Thighs turn me on tremendously. Not that they have to be beautiful. It's not the visual. When I get attracted to someone, that's the first fantasy that comes to me. I'll be sitting and talking to her, and I'll be thinking how I really want to wrap my legs around her thighs."

Kathy worships collarbones: "I love kissing my lover's shoulders and then those indents right on either side of her neck. We call them 'kiss cups.'"

Jenn loves everything: "My main thing is thighs. And I like butts. Toes. Ears. Nipples. Eyes."

So does Suzanne: "I love my lover's butt. I love hands, arms, muscles, breasts. Arches of feet. And toes. And backs of knees. And breasts, definitely. Legs, insides of thighs, insides of elbows. Skin. The whole body is an erogenous zone."

BODY ART. For some women, body art has become an exciting sexual trend. Many lesbians sport tattoos; pierced nipples, labia, and eyebrows are not uncommon. One woman explained that having her tongue pierced felt both sexual and spiritual, and her girlfriend agreed that it added spice to their kissing. On the other hand, many women are horrified by body art and shudder at the idea of having sex with someone who has a picture on her breast or a ring in her labia.

A wonderful and sometimes intimidating fact about lesbians is that you cannot easily predict who will be radical and who will be conservative — or even what those terms mean. It would seem safe to guess that the young queer woman in leather is more apt to have a pierced nipple or tattooed shoulder than the older lesbian in an elegant dress, but you never know.

If you choose to have body art done, make sure the tattooer or piercer is absolutely trustworthy and that the circumstances are totally hygienic. Professional body artists can usually be found in large metropolitan areas; some do tours. *On Our Backs* has many ads for body art practitioners.

BODY IMAGE. Many lesbians, big and small, worry about their weight and dislike parts of their bodies. Welcome to the real world, where Lane Bryant's five-foot-nine, 155-pound model is called "large-sized"; where TV and movies glorify women with body fat percentages usually seen in the ill and the starving; and where girls start dieting in the second grade and despair when they grow up. Add in breast augmentation operations, and the "ideal women's body" is presented as that of a young boy sporting giant, gravity-defying breasts.

Although lesbians often break away from mainstream assumptions and expectations, we would have to move to Mars to escape the message that having a female shape means that we have somewhere, somehow, done something wrong. In addition, incest, rape, sexism, and other forms of abuse often scar the survivor's self-image. As a result, many lesbians suffer from anorexia and bulimia (anorexic women limit their intake of food severely, sometimes to the point of starvation; bulimic women binge and then make themselves vomit the food they have eaten), and few of us are genuinely pleased with our bodies.

Being overweight isn't the only fear women experience about our bodies. Some feel flat-chested; others worry about the shapes of their legs or arms or bellies.

Of the women interviewed for this book, only two expressed any consistent pleasure with their physical wrappings. Jessica says, "I've always really liked my body. I'm fortunate because I fit into the stereotypical idea of what women's bodies are supposed to be like in our society. I'm slim and tall."

Gail is a big African-American lesbian, so she has had to contend with multiple prejudices about what makes a woman attractive; in addition, she is an incest survivor. However, she has a positive self-image: "It's something that evolved. For years, because of being a survivor, I was detached from my body, but now I'm comfortable. I think karate has helped. I think dancing has helped. And being active in sports. Basketball and going to the gym. Riding my bike. Working up a sweat in general. But the conditioning is so insidious that it's hard to completely eradicate it. So while I am comfortable to some degree, there are still little corners that could be swept out."

Interestingly enough, while many women despair about their own bodies, they welcome variety in their lovers. For Suzanne, the only definite appearance no-no is "geeky shoes." Kathy says her lovers have ranged from "five-foot-ten and 115 pounds to five-foot-four and 190 — and they were all attractive." Jessica revels in choice: "One great thing about being a lesbian is that there are so many different bodies to love." All the interviewees found attitude more important than looks.

If you're new to the lesbian world, you may find that your attractiveness is more appreciated here than in mainstream society. Kathy says, "In the straight community, I'm an overweight, short-haired, middle-aged woman, but in the lesbian community, I'm cute!"

If you feel bad about your physical self, you may want to check out *Lesbian Sex,* by JoAnn Loulan, which offers "homework exercises" to help you reclaim your body, plus *The Beauty Myth,* by Naomi Wolf, which discusses how lifelong anti-body brainwashing occurs. If you suffer from anorexia or bulimia, it's important that you seek therapy or a support group; otherwise, you may permanently damage your health.

BONDAGE. Even women who claim no interest in S/M often enjoy using bondage and blindfolds during sex. Bondage frees the tied-up woman from responsibility and allows her to be totally open to the experience her partner provides. Blindfolds add a touch of mystery and suspense; many women start tingling just from wondering where they will be touched next. The combination of bondage and blindfolds encourages complete receptivity.

Don't let anyone tie you up unless you trust her absolutely. The trust must be threefold: that she won't hurt you (unless you want her to, in which case see *Sadomasochism);* that she will untie you if you ask her to; and that she knows what she is doing. Nor should you tie someone up unless you are absolutely, 110 percent sure she wants you to *and* you have some knowledge of knots and safety measures.

If part of your fun is to struggle and resist, you and your partner should pick a "safeword" to signal that you are not enjoying yourself anymore. Many women use "red" to mean stop, while "pink" signifies "less, please." Establishing these words leaves you safe to yell "no, no, no" to your heart's content.

Take time to learn something about bondage before adding it to your sex life. Experiment with different materials and knots. Avoid silk; although it seems sexy, it allows knots to tighten dangerously. Make sure that two or three fingers can fit between the restraint and the body of the tied-up woman. Don't tie your partner's hands over her head for extended lengths of time, and don't tether her so that she is hanging without her feet firmly on the floor. Keep a pair of scissors nearby so that the bonds can be cut quickly in case of emergency. When using handcuffs or other locks, keep the keys close at hand.

There are many positions in which someone can be restrained. Some women prefer being tied spread-eagled lying down, while others enjoy standing up with their hands tied behind their backs. Take the time to find which options you both fancy. Also experiment with amounts of restraint. While some women prefer loose restraints that are more symbolic than real, others like to be stretched out and truly immobilized. Some women relish fighting their bonds, while others enjoy just staying still.

BONOBOS. One of the favorite "reasons" homophobes offer for hating lesbians and gay men is that "homosexuality is unnatural; it doesn't exist in nature." That's what they claim, anyway. In reality, homosexuality occurs *everywhere* in nature (see also *Kinsey Report*). One species in which homosexual behavior plays a particularly important role is the bonobo.

Bonobos, also known as "pygmy chimps," are fruit-eating apes found in Zaire. According to *Natural History* and *Discover* magazines, bonobos are not actually small chimpanzees; the two species diverged some 1.5 to 2 million years ago. Humans are believed to have shared a common ancestor with bonobos some 3 million years before that.

Bonobos differ from chimps in significant ways. For instance, while male chimps sometimes murder chimp infants, bonobos never seem to kill members of their own species. In addition, chimp females can only refuse sex from males smaller than they are, with the result that chimp rape is common; female bonobos, however, can turn down males, and often do. In general, bonobos are more peaceful than chimps.

How do researchers explain the amiability of the bonobos?

Bonobos love to fuck!

When bonobos are faced with tension, they all start having sex with each other. For example, many species dealing with a limited food supply fight over what food is available, but bonobos become down-right orgiastic — females with females, males with males, and mixed couples. In this way, they re-establish their connections and dissipate their tensions. A female joining a group of females who are already eating will rub genitals with each of them before beginning to feed. In

Natural History, Takayoshi Kano, who has studied bonobos for decades, writes that, "To all appearances, these behaviors evoke shared sexual excitement and great erotic pleasure."

Some female bonobos have special girlfriends. *Discover* magazine tells of two female bonobos at the San Diego Wild Animal Park who ignored a male bonobo's request for sex, then went behind a tree and rubbed their genitals together.

So here we have a species in which rampant homo- and heterosexuality improves the life of its members. It is a species with relatively little fighting and no murder. In addition, the females get to pick whom they have sex with. No wonder the homophobes don't want to hear about sexual variety in nature!

BOOKS. Many coming-out tales begin with a trip to the library. Unfortunately, as recently as the 1960s and into the 1970s, nascent lesbians would discover through books that they were inverted, perverted, sick, or abnormal. But the world of publishing has traveled light years since then, mostly through the efforts of lesbian and gay presses. The newly out woman today can turn to books from Naiad Press, Spinsters, Aunt Lute, Alyson Publications, Cleis, Paradigm Books, and many others. In addition, mainstream publishers now publish some lesbian history and fiction.

Books can help you discover the particular ways you want to be sexual. In nonfiction, Joan Nestle's *The Persistent Desire* and JoAnn Loulan's *The Lesbian Erotic Dance* focus on butch/femme roles. Susie Bright shares her unique point of view about everything from vibrators to piercing in *Susie Sexpert's Lesbian Sex World* and *Susie Bright's Sexual Reality.* Samois's *Coming to Power* thoroughly explores S/M sexuality.

Fiction can offer as much sexual information as nonfiction. Many lesbian novels have extended sex scenes that show all the different ways women make love together.

There are also lesbian-specific books about coming out, legal matters, having children, health, and even fixing your motorcycle. (See also the *Resource List.*)

BREAKING UP. See *Rebound Relationships; Rejection.*

BREAST SELF-EXAMINATION. In a world filled with mixed messages, it's nice to know there are occasional straightforward facts. Here's one: doing a monthly breast self-examination (BSE) can save your life.

The best time to examine your breasts is at the end of your menstrual cycle, when they are the least swollen. If you don't menstruate, check your breasts the first of every month or on some other easily remembered day.

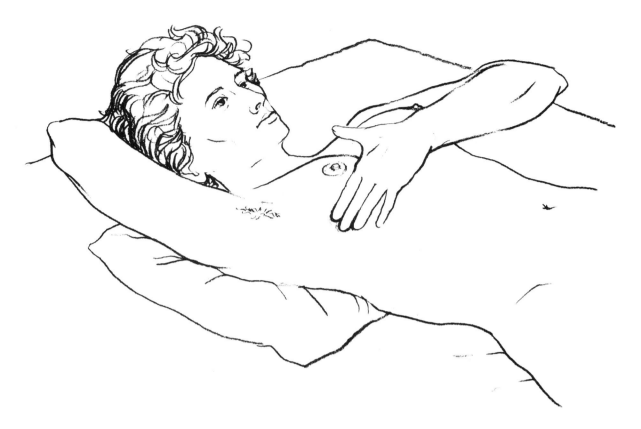

Start by facing yourself in a mirror, leaning forward, with your shoulders hunched toward each other. Examine your breasts visually in the mirror, looking for lumps, puckers, and odd coloration. Check your nipples for discharge or color changes. Also examine the areas around your breasts, including your armpits. Repeat the visual examination standing up straight.

Then lie down on your back. Place a pillow under your shoulder on the same side as the breast you are examining. Feel under your armpits for lumps. Using three fingers, palpate your breast; that is, touch it slowly and methodically, either in strips up and down (or back and forth) or pie slices. Do not lift your fingers from your breast, as you may lose your place. Lotion on your fingers will help you to slide them around your breasts more easily.

If your breasts are large, palpate each area with a few different pressures (gentle, medium, and firm) to feel the different levels of breast tissue beneath your fingers. During your first BSEs, endeavor to learn the texture of your breasts so well that you can detect any future changes that occur. It's helpful to draw a map of your breast that includes the locations of any swellings or areas that feel different or odd.

Many women have lumps in their breasts all the time; if you have just started doing BSEs and you find something, have your doctor make sure that it's not dangerous. While at the doctor's office, have her watch how you do your BSE and suggest improvements in your technique. Also have the doctor explain exactly what a suspicious lump feels like. Women who receive feedback on their BSE technique are more likely to do BSEs regularly and efficiently than those who depend on written instructions. In addition, many video rental stores carry BSE instructional tapes.

Actually finding a lump can be quite frightening. But, while you're in the doctor's waiting room biting your nails, remember: the vast majority of lumps are not cancerous.

BREASTS. Lesbian lore claims that women make perfect love to other women because "they know how their partners feel since they feel the same way."

Another bit of conventional wisdom bites the dust.

Breasts are as individual as their owners. Not only do they differ in size and shape, but they also differ in sensitivity. Some women couldn't care less about having their breasts stimulated; some dislike having them touched at all. Other women adore having their breasts stroked and licked and nibbled, and the occasional woman can even reach orgasm from breast arousal. To discover your partner's preferences, either pay careful attention to her responses to what you do, or ask her. Perhaps you two can explore her likes and dislikes together.

There are many ways to pleasure breasts. You might cup one of her breasts in both hands, or have one hand on each breast. Stroke or knead them gently, or not so gently. Kiss and nibble the breasts, perhaps occasionally teasing her by barely touching the nipple. Rub your breasts against hers. Switch your mouth back and forth from one breast to the other. Vary pressures and speeds. However, don't keep changing from one form of stimulation to another; when you find one that works, give her time to enjoy it.

Most women prefer that you not go immediately for their nipples — and when you do, that you start gently. Once you have been stimulating her nipples for a while, try building the pressure and speed of what you're doing. Often, nipples that are shy at first can be ravenous for attention a few minutes later, although some never desire more than a tender kiss or two.

Nipples respond to a wide variety of approaches. Pinch her nipple gently, or roll it between your fingers, perhaps tugging slightly as you do so. Lick across its top or around it in circles. Suck her nipple into your mouth, or use your tongue to push it inverted into her breast. Kiss and suck her at the same time, pulling gently away from her body. Focus on one nipple with your mouth while caressing the other breast with your hand.

If her breasts are large, it may be possible to squeeze them together so that you can lick both nipples at the same time. Or find a position where you can play with her breasts while she plays with yours.

She'll enjoy some of these approaches more than others, of course, but they're all worth trying over time.

BUTCH/FEMME. Defining butch/femme is not easy. Even the most eloquent of women tend toward sentences such as, "I know a femme when I see one," or "I can spot a butch at fifty yards" — without explaining how they can tell who is butch and who is femme.

JoAnn Loulan's *The Lesbian Erotic Dance* sheds some light on definitions. According to Loulan's research, femmes describe butches as athletic, handsome, hard, and lean, while butches describe femmes as curvy, delicate, elegant, and pretty. However, both butches *and* femmes are considered aggressive, assertive, beautiful, independent, sexy, and strong, so there is some overlap.

Some women claim that butch/femme identities rely on male and female models, but self-identified butches and femmes insist that they do not imitate heterosexuals, nor do they play roles. Butch/femme is a way of living and of being sexual.

A detailed examination of butch/femme is beyond the scope of this book; *The Persistent Desire*, edited by Joan Nestle, takes close to five hundred pages to discuss the topic, and it's a must-read for anyone interested in butch/femme identities or in lesbian history.

For the newly out lesbian, the most important thing to know about butch/femme is that it is an orientation, just as being a lesbian is an orientation. If you embrace it, you may get some grief from lesbians who consider it "outdated," but don't let anyone prevent you from expressing who you are. Stopping yourself from being butch or femme may be as destructive as stopping yourself from sleeping with women.

On the other hand, if butch/femme doesn't appeal to you, don't pursue it. Be aware, however, that you may find yourself being labeled butch or femme anyway, even by women who claim they aren't into roles!

You may also find that the lesbian community values butchy women more than femmes, perhaps as a result of internalized sexism. This preference even exists outside the butch/femme world. As Rebecca sums it up, "Lots of women don't believe in roles, but they know they're not femmes." According to butch/femme dilettantes, butch equals competent; butch equals strong; butch equals intelligent. No wonder butches are valued more highly than femmes! Yet most women who take butch/femme seriously disagree with these equations.

The best way to deal with butch/femme is to be who you are and let others be who they are. (See also *Who's On Top?)*

BUTTS. Lesbian butts are great fun. They can be squeezed and bitten and licked and kissed, and they look great in jeans or pants suits or skirts or dresses. If you want to be sure to pleasure someone, massage her butt. It may be the only physical thing that *everyone* on earth enjoys.

BUTT PLUGS. See *Dildos and Butt Plugs*.

C

CASUAL SEX. (Any sex in which the participants seek sexual pleasure only, with no plans for a relationship; includes friendly affairs, one-night stands, and anonymous sex.)

The capacity to enjoy casual sex varies from individual to individual. Lydia says, "Right now, most of the people I'm sexually involved with are friends. I think my ability to do this has come from practice." Lydia also once tried sex with a stranger and enjoyed herself tremendously, although she found that they were unable to repeat the experience.

Kathy has tried friendly affairs, with some success. In one case, "I was trying to recover from a bad breakup, and it was great to have someone to sleep with. She gave me my sexual confidence back. And we had fun!" But her one time with a stranger was a total disaster. "I hated it."

Jenn is a wholehearted sexual adventurer: "Once I slept with an ex-lover because I knew the sex would be good and there'd be no strings. And once two women picked me up hitchhiking, and I went home and partied with them. It was a really neat experience. Another time, in San Francisco, I went home with a woman I met at a bar. I had an absolute blast."

Suzanne has never slept with a stranger, although she's considered casual sex with good friends and ex-lovers: "There have been times I've wanted to, but we weren't both comfortable or it was too scary. Or we were afraid we'd fuck up the friendship."

Rebecca has had sex with an ex-lover, but "I found it very sad. It reminded me of what used to be." Her one attempt at sex with someone she barely knew "was a bad experience. I really need romance in my sex. That's what turns me on."

Gail likes casual sex with her exes. "The funny thing is, there's usually this tremendous passion between us. And there's an understanding that this means *only* that we enjoy each other sexually." The one time she tried anonymous sex, she found she didn't want to do more than cuddle.

Should you choose to have sex with a stranger, be careful. Consider practicing safer sex; Alice knows a woman whose *one* anonymous experience left her with a lifelong case of herpes. And if you have casual sex with an ex-lover or a friend, make sure the boundaries are carefully drawn and understood by both of you.

Casual sex is most likely to work for you if you acknowledge what you really want. If you seek affection or love, sex with a stranger will be unfulfilling — and even painful. If you try casual sex with a friend, it may be difficult *not* to fall in love. Either way, the loneliness you felt before may be doubled afterward, and your needs would be better met by going dancing or to the movies with some buddies.

But, for all the risks inherent in casual sex, it should probably occur *more* frequently among women. Lesbians often believe we must marry everyone we sleep with, resulting in too many painful, pointless relationships. For women who don't want to get involved, perhaps because they are focused on getting a degree or aren't emotionally ready or just don't want a relationship, friendly affairs can satisfy sexual needs. Sometimes a woman just wants to get laid! Sex needn't be paid for with marriage vows.

Base your sexual habits on who you are and what you want. Not what your parents want you to want, not what your religious leaders teach you to want, not what the TV tells you to want, and not what the current lesbian fad insists that you want. If you discover monogamy is the only way for you, hold out for monogamy. If you want to experiment, experiment. If you want only to have casual sex for your whole life, then only have casual sex. Whatever road you take, the journey will be easier if it's *your* journey.

CELIBACY. At various times in our lives, we may choose to stay celibate for a while. Some women masturbate during these periods; others practice absolute abstinence.

Periods of celibacy offer unparalleled opportunities for growth and self-exploration, during which a woman may focus on incest work in therapy, complete a particular project, recover from a bad breakup, or prove to herself that she can survive without a lover.

Being celibate can be frightening, particularly for women who habitually drown their problems and sorrows in sex and relationships. But celibacy almost invariably turns out to be productive and self-affirming, recharging a woman's batteries and changing her view of the world.

Kathy says, "I was mostly celibate for eleven months, with a couple of one-night stands. It was my first time without a full-time lover in eight years! When I did get involved with someone, it was because I wanted *her,* not because I had to be in a relationship. Taking time off was one of the best gifts I ever gave myself."

Gail turned her celibacy experience into performance art: "I had not been happy that I was choosing partners who had difficulties with intimacy. And I realized we all have problems with intimacy. So I felt like I needed to take a break from relationships, just to cultivate the one with myself. I did that for a year. On my one-year anniversary, I had a celebration. I invited people to bring passion foods of their choosing, and I told my guests that they could not come through the door unless they brought a poem or something to share. We talked about sex and sensuality. I emphasized that just because you choose not to be sexual with someone, it doesn't mean that you aren't a sensual, sexual being. It was a very wonderful evening."

Rebecca sums up her celibate period by saying, "It helped me a lot. I learned that there are things I depend on a lover for that I can find in myself or with other people in other ways."

CHILDREN. Despite myths to the contrary, many lesbians have children, and not always from previous heterosexual relationships. So many gay women are getting artificially inseminated (with either anonymous sperm or donations from friends) that we have a slang term for their children, based on a favored mode of sperm delivery: "turkey-baster babies."

Dealing with your children. For women who already have children when they come out of the closet, dealing with the kids' responses to their lesbianism will be a *big deal.* Although some children react well to learning the news, others freak out that their mom is "weird." This response is not surprising; in many schoolyards, the absolutely worst insults center around homosexuality. In addition, the children may still be reeling from their parents' divorce. For teenagers, who generally crave fitting in more than anything else, finding out that Mom loves a woman feels like doomsday.

The biggest challenge comes when Mom's female lover moves in with her and the kids. The usual pressures of introducing someone new into a family unit become multiplied by the shame and anger the kids may feel that their mom is gay.

Many kids eventually become accepting and even proud of their lesbian mothers, although some never do. However, no matter how upset the kids are, the mother still has every right to express her sexual orientation. After all, the children will not be better off if she is miserable and resentful, and *all* children must someday learn that their folks are people too.

To keep their love life relaxed and uninterrupted, the lesbian mother and her partner may choose, whenever possible, to have sex when the children aren't home. One mother spoke of her secret pleasure when her daughter asked if she could stay at a friend's house for the weekend. "If you do all your chores," the mother replied evenly, then danced for joy at the idea of two days alone with her lover.

Unfortunately, some lesbians hate dealing with their lover's kids, and the lesbian mother may feel pulled between her children and her lover. This can particularly be a problem when the lover has no

personal interest in being a parent. If the women choose to stay together, the usual tools will come in handy: communication, compromise, and a sense of humor.

In the loveliest scenario, and it does happen, the mother's partner grows to love and be loved by the children, and a beautiful new family is born.

Rip Corley's book, *The Final Closet,* offers advice to lesbian and gay parents about coming out to their offspring.

Having kids after you're out. There are a million ramifications to having a baby, particularly when you're a lesbian. *Considering Parenthood,* by Cheri Pies, discusses lesbian motherhood, whether adoptive or biological, at length, including legal, emotional, and medical considerations.

Some pregnant women forget about sex altogether. Once the child is born (or the adopted child is brought home), the standard problems of sleep deprivation and stress set in, and the mother may have no interest in sex for a while.

On the other hand, Susie Bright, in *Susie Bright's Sexual Reality,* demonstrates the full possible extent of a woman's sexuality during both pregnancy and early motherhood. Bright believes that few women actually stop wanting sex; she suggests finding fresh ways to make love that take into account body changes and new life demands.

One way or another, pregnancy and new motherhood do change a person's sex life. For the woman in a relationship, particularly if she *doesn't* want sex, dealing with her partner's needs may take extra communication and negotiation. If both partners consider the child to be *theirs,* compromising will be easier.

Bringing up children in a lesbian home. Lesbian parents need to be prepared to explain their lives to their children and to support the kids when classmates are judgmental and nasty; the children of gay parents may also suffer a sense of isolation as they look around them in school and on TV and see only heterosexuality. Books like *Heather Has Two Mommies, Gloria Goes to Gay Pride,* and *The Duke Who Outlawed Jelly Beans and Other Stories* can help very young children to see they are not alone, and hanging out with other gay-parented families provides both parents and kids with friends who understand what they are going through.

CHOICE. You have the right to say yes or no to sex. You have the right to say yes or no to relationships. You have only one life at a time, but you can pick which one.

CIVIL RIGHTS. See *History; Legal Matters.*

CLASS. It is not surprising that cross-class relationships are frequent in the lesbian community. Straight people can socialize according to finances, interests, and habits, generally meeting other people like themselves, but lesbians from diverse backgrounds must squeeze into the few bars, support groups, and organizations available in any given region. Teachers and sailors, garage mechanics and social workers, executives and cops all hang out together, and some of them fall in love.

This is not to say that classism is unknown in the lesbian community. Unfortunately, it is alive and well in some quarters, cutting in many directions. "Professional women" may set restrictive dress codes for their events, keeping out poorer women. Lower-income women may establish boundaries by harshly criticizing women who make money. One lesbian vice president said, "When I go to a dyke party, I leave home the BMW and take the pickup truck. Otherwise, women yell at me."

While classism is a pointless prejudice in any community, it is particularly toxic in the lesbian world. There are too few lesbians for us to split into still smaller groups. In addition, classism breeds misinformation. For instance, classist assumptions might lead someone to think that working-class women are more likely than rich women to have tattoos and pierced labia. Or that executives and businesswomen have never abused intravenous drugs. Or that certain "types" of women would be more likely to practice S/M sex. But these assumptions are inaccurate, and dangerous too.

The characteristics of lesbians in a particular class are hard to predict because unexpected changes occur in women who survive the coming-out process. After realizing that the whole world was wrong about lesbianism, we wonder what else the world was wrong about. We may start to question *everything* and explore parts of ourselves we would have ignored had we stayed in the straight world.

Once people have started exploring, we settle into our *own* preferences, and very often those preferences cannot be predicted by class, race, upbringing, or appearance. *Nor can HIV status ever be predicted from class, race, upbringing, or appearance.*

It's true: you can't judge a book by its cover.

CLEANLINESS. With the exception of those few women who prefer literally down-and-dirty sex, most lesbians enjoy making love with a partner who is clean. While douching is not necessary (and can upset the usual balance of yeast and bacteria living in the vagina), showering or bathing regularly is.

Some attempts at smelling good can backfire; deodorants taste terrible during armpit burrowing, and perfumes can set off a partner's allergies. However, many women do use deodorants, and a simple warning to your sex partner can save her from getting a mouthful of metallic yick.

The easiest way to guarantee both your cleanliness and hers is to suggest a shower or bath as sexual foreplay. Stroking each other with soap-slippery hands will turn you on while you achieve cleanliness and confidence.

CLITORIS. Okay, you're ready to have sex with someone new. She's attractive, fun, and easy to talk to. You bravely decide to discuss your sexual preferences and fears before actually making love, but you quickly hit a stumbling block: how the hell do you pronounce *clitoris*?

There are two recognized pronunciations: one sounds rather like "hit or miss" and the other is useful for limericks about women named Dolores. Both sound rather awful, although the "hit or miss" version is more popular among lesbians. For the record, the word comes from the Greek *kleitoris* or "small hill."

The visible part of the clitoris, which varies in size from woman to woman, is only the tip of the iceberg. However, the total extent of the entire clitoris is a topic of debate. By some accounts, it is an inch or so long, extending up and into a woman's body. By others, the clitoris is "all the structures that function together to produce orgasm," including the inner lips, the hood, the urethral sponge, various muscles in the area, and much more (check out the book *A New View of a Woman's Body* for further details).

Whatever the definition, the clitoris is a highly innervated structure that becomes erect with sexual arousal. For many women, the only route to orgasm is through clitoral stimulation (see also *Anatomy; Orgasms; Vaginal Orgasms*).

Clitorises have as many personalities as their owners. Some like hard stimulation, while others prefer gentleness. Some like to be touched directly, while others prefer to be stroked through the labia or slightly to the side. Getting to know your clitoris and your partner's is one of the delights of sex.

CLOTHES. Contemporary lesbians wear an unlimited range of clothing. Day-to-day wear includes business suits, jeans and t-shirts, leather pants and jackets, tailored trousers and silk blouses, tights and long shirts, and slinky dresses and heels. Underwear also varies from woman to woman, with some lesbians choosing lace and silk and others wearing Jockey for Her or even men's boxer shorts.

How a woman dresses depends on her personal tastes, how she makes a living, and how much money she can or chooses to devote to clothing. There is no single lesbian uniform, no right way to dress. There is also no clothing that automatically makes a woman attractive

— or unattractive — to lesbians. (See also *Appearances; Butch/Femme; Costumes and Uniforms.*)

COMING OUT. Coming out is a lifelong process with social, sexual, spiritual, and emotional components. The main goal of coming out is to replace internalized homophobia with self-acceptance and pride. This change relates to sexuality in a fundamental way: few people can have fulfilling, passionate sex lives while feeling bad about themselves.

The most important person a lesbian must come out to is herself. Some women have "always known" they were gay; others gradually recognize their orientation after years of heterosexual marriage. Rarely does a lesbian instantly and comfortably accept her sexuality; more often, she spends years searching, reading, talking to friends, and experimenting before she can jettison the belief system that says lesbians are abnormal, disgusting, and perverted.

For some women, coming out includes questioning *all* their beliefs, and they may end up more radical and more angry than they ever expected. Others embrace their sexuality without altering their politics and world view.

Coming out to friends and family. While a lesbian may choose to keep her sexual orientation secret from all but a lover and a friend or two, many gay women come out to their friends, families, and co-workers — and sometimes to the whole world.

Depending on her loved ones' beliefs and personalities, the woman who comes out may experience quick acceptance, total rejection, or any response in between. Some friends will need time to digest the news; others may never speak to her again. And a surprising number may say, "We were wondering when you'd finally tell us!"

Although exhausting and frightening, coming out is necessary for full and happy relationships with friends and family. Jean Genet said, "It is better to be hated for what you are than loved for what you are not," and while his aphorism may seem extreme, there is much truth to it. Fortunately, with changing societal mores, gay people are getting to be loved for who they *are* — certainly the best of all possible worlds.

The lesbian who chooses secrecy, whether because she works for a homophobic employer, teaches school, or just feels unsafe coming out, can end up lonely and frightened, often with good reason. Scared to be honest, hiding her true self, the closeted lesbian often internalizes her situation as meaning there *is* something wrong with her. But there isn't. Even if the entire military establishment and the major religions all claim homosexuality is wrong, *it is they who are wrong.* But this is hard to remember without support. The woman with an extended social system of lesbians, gay men, and open straight people will more easily overcome internalized homophobia and learn to love herself than the woman in the closet.

Coming out also educates the gay woman's straight friends that lesbians are nice people, just like her and just like them.

Most importantly, as Rebecca explains, coming out is liberating: "I'm so grateful I became a lesbian. I was thirty-six before I came out, and I hate the thought that I could have spent my whole life and missed this! I just thank my higher power, or whatever you want to call it."

Warning: If you live with your folks, don't come out to them unless you are sure you can support yourself; too many parents kick out their gay children. Similarly, if you want to come out at work, be sure you have a backup way to make a living should you get fired. Unfortunately, in most places, you will have no recourse if you get canned for being gay. And never assume you know how any particular person will respond to your news; many lesbians and gay men have been shocked at the unexpected negative *and* positive reactions they've experienced.

On the other hand, don't be so cautious that you never take a chance. The closet is a very lonely place.

Two books that may help you find your way through the coming-out process are *Coming Out: An Act of Love* and *Coming Out to Parents*.

Finding a place in the lesbian community. Although some women are happy to know few lesbians other than their lover, many seek a community in which to socialize and form family bonds. This search can take much time and effort; for women from rural areas, it may include moving to a large city. There are many benefits offered by places like San Francisco and New York that are not available in most other locations, including support groups, a variety of bars, social groups, 12-step meetings, sports leagues, and political organizations specifically for lesbians or lesbians and gay men. On the other hand, lesbians from smaller cities and rural areas sometimes find that their communities are stronger and more cohesive than those in larger cities, since they know that, with their small numbers, they must stick together.

The section *Meeting People* discusses how to find the lesbian community.

The first lesbians you find will not reflect *all* lesbians. If you're taking your earliest tentative steps into the community, you may want to run away when you see "what lesbians look like" (depending on the era, "what lesbians look like" has included everything from work shirts and jeans to leather, lipstick, and pierced eyebrows). It's easy to see one group of women and feel that you're not like them; they dress funny, or they're too masculine, or too loud, or whatever. Since you've grown up with the antilesbian stereotypes of mainstream culture, you may glance past average-looking women to the most extremely clad ones, then mistakenly decide that the latter are the "real lesbians."

On looking closer and meeting more women, you will see that "what lesbians look like" is what all women look like. Some are big, some are small; some dress sloppily, others wear only the finest clothing; some have cropped hair, others have flowing tresses. And while you may be relieved to see that many lesbians look "normal," as time goes on you'll probably find yourself appreciating more and more variation in lesbian styles. One day, those "extremely clad" lesbians may just look great!

Just as there is variety in lesbian styles, there is also variety in lesbian personalities. Lesbians do all sorts of jobs, have all sorts of belief systems, enjoy all sorts of hobbies, and vary in our sexual habits in all sorts of ways. As you come further and further out of the closet, you will find lesbians you adore and some you just don't like. You will also find lovely sex partners and potential long-term lovers. The woman of your dreams may be just around the corner — and you will be better able to enjoy her as you grow more and more comfortable with your own sexuality.

COMMUNICATION. Communication tops the list of the traits most important to good sex (and to good relationships). Contrary to sex scenes in movies — where lovers instinctively know each other's every desire in displays of mind-reading that could win them jobs as psychics — real people have varying needs and occasionally undecipherable moods. The best way to exchange information is to talk to each other!

Not that every sexual movement needs to be planned, discussed, and certified by both partners before the first kiss can take place. But the sooner you are comfortable talking to each other, the sooner you will feel safe to gasp, "faster," "softer," or "slightly to the left" when you want to. And it really is okay, even recommended, to talk with someone before you go to bed with her.

Good communication can unfold naturally between two people, or you may choose a more formal approach. Start with a discussion of what vocabulary you prefer. Even if you've already had sex together, you may find it surprisingly difficult to name places you have just been touching and licking. Unfortunately, English lacks a useful vocabulary for sex; in addition, most of us don't have much experience saying "those words" out loud unless we're cursing or telling dirty jokes.

To help you both feel safe in revealing your sexual vocabulary and needs, set some guidelines. Negativity and judgment have no place in this sort of conversation. If you have a problem with a certain word or act, say, "Well, I don't feel good about that." Don't say, "That's disgusting," or "That's male-identified and you wouldn't say that if you were a real lesbian," or "You must be kidding!" — even if the idea put forth is so repugnant that you no longer want to have sex with her.

And, yes, that can happen. If you are into vanilla sex and she insists on rocky road, you may never reach a common ground where you can both enjoy yourselves. In such cases, honest communication will save you from spending days, weeks, or even years of your lives searching for something that just isn't there.

Communication must have limits, too. Don't feel obliged to discuss topics that make you uneasy. This is conversation, not a contest or an exam. For many women, talking about sexual desire is a new and frightening idea, and you and your partner may prefer to go slowly. It's a rare pair of humans who achieve perfect communication the first time they try, just as it's a rare pair who achieve perfect sex the first time they try.

The idea of talking *during* sex may rub some people the wrong way, but many women find it adds to the experience. Jessica says, "I always ask, 'Is this okay?' I don't just assume that she loves what I'm doing. And I feel safest when she does the same thing with me. I slept with one woman who said, 'Take me,' and I thought, 'Ooh, I feel like I'm in a romance novel.' And there was a woman who said she'd like to be 'inside' me, and that was absolutely wonderful."

Framing comments positively is even more important during sex than beforehand. If it sounds like you're directing traffic, your partner may get turned off or annoyed. Snapping, "You're doing me too hard!" will not improve the moment. On the other hand, "Oh, honey, I love it when you fuck me slow and gentle" provides information plus its own sexual thrill.

Communicating about sex need not be limited to your partner. By talking with friends, you can learn new approaches, receive support to try new techniques, and gain reassurance that you're not the only one who gets scared, brazen, shy, just not in the mood, ravenous — or whatever — during sex.

The hunger for sexual information is large in the lesbian community; as a matter of fact, Rebecca believes that part of the attraction of S/M for many lesbians is that S/M women "are the only group of lesbians talking about sex. And S/M is a structured way to feel safe to do what you want to do. It has scene setting and guidelines. You can play out your fantasy — though mine wouldn't be an S/M fantasy! We need non-S/M groups that offer the information, the scene setting, the structure, the guidelines, and the talking about fantasies."

COMPATIBILITY. Compatibility is right up there with communication on the list of necessities for good sex and, particularly, for good relationships.

Sex. In sex between women, compatibility may seem to be a given, but it's not. Far from it. Lesbians prefer their lovemaking soft or hard, fast or slow, oral or digital, morning or night, lights on or lights off, silent or noisy, silly or serious, and various combinations thereof.

Minor disagreements are no problem; after all, you can make love in the morning sometimes and in the evening other times. But what if one woman craves being tied up and the other is vanilla all the way? What if one considers penetration male-identified and therefore disgusting and the other just wants to get fucked? It may not be possible to resolve these differences except, perhaps, for a brief affair.

But no one is wrong! With some care and consideration, you may switch from being lovers to being friends and still enjoy the feelings you have for each other. Passion doesn't only exist in sex; ardent friendships are a boon in anyone's life.

On the other hand, if you two are compatible, your road to pleasure is that much smoother. It doesn't matter if you want sex once an hour or once a year. You can indulge in the hardest-core S/M or the sweetest vanilla. Perhaps neither of you likes oral sex. As long as you agree, what does it matter? You can pleasure yourselves on your own terms.

Relationships. Long-term relationships usually demand more than sexual compatibility. Do you have similar goals in life? Do you enjoy at least some of the same pastimes? Do your views about money mesh? Are you both comfortable in the closet — or out of it? Can you handle each other's levels of cleanliness or messiness?

Some of these compatibility issues outweigh others, and everyone knows a couple or two who seem to have nothing in common. But a closer look often reveals shared values or shared hobbies — or maybe they're so hot together in bed that they don't care about *anything* else.

Kathy's lover is a slender jock, while Kathy resents that she can't lose weight while eating all the chocolate she wants. Her lover is an introvert, while Kathy is an extrovert. Friends have commented that they seem an odd pair. But they share a love of reading, taking long drives, and cuddling. They both lean toward leftist politics, and they both avoid doing the dishes. Their sexual tastes follow a similar continuum of vanilla to mint chocolate chip, and they long ago decided how to share their money. And they both find their relationship delightful.

No two people are identical, nor do any two people share the exact same values. But if two women don't agree on the important things, their life together, sexual and romantic, will start with two strikes against it.

CONSENT. Sex without the full consent of both partners is rape.

COSTUMES AND UNIFORMS. Costumes can add an extra dimension to sex. Military uniforms turn on many lesbians, while tight leather skirts with fishnet stockings cause others to melt.

Lydia enjoys a range of costuming: "I'm getting into leather jackets and chaps, but I'm also getting into lingerie. I have a bustiere and a teddy. Dressing up really does set the mood." Gail remembers, "My ex and I fantasized about her being a construction worker. She had the garb, so she wore the belt and boots and jeans and hat, and that was fun." Suzanne and Kathy have both enjoyed sexual experiences with lovers who wore a leather jacket and nothing else; Suzanne says, "I think combinations of covering and uncovering are really exciting." Jessica loves "unbuttoning a man's shirt on a woman, and having breasts come out." And Kathy has a friend who dreams of making love with a nurse who's wearing a starched white uniform and a little white cap.

If you've got the interest and the money, you can buy wonderful sex clothing from Frederick's of Hollywood, Stormy Leather, or even Victoria's Secret or Lane Bryant. For a cheaper approach, dig through your closets and see what you come up with. Something as simple as a skirt worn with no underwear can be a huge turn-on.

CRUSHES. Throughout our lives we experience crushes, and how they affect us depends on how we respond to them. Teenage crushes on our female best friends can be heartbreaking, especially when our feelings are dismissed as "a phase" and those wonderful girls start dating jerky guys who don't treat them half as well as we would!

Crushes are more fun in the lesbian world since we can act on them. But they're also fun when we don't. Since lesbians choose their lovers and friends from the same pool of people, it is not unusual for good friends to experience some sexual tension, and that extra frisson adds luster to the friendship even while you both stay faithful to your lovers.

It's also fun to have crushes on movie stars, co-workers, and even male friends, particularly if *crush* is defined as admiration plus a touch of attraction. But if a crush on someone you can't have turns to love or obsession, it may become considerably less pleasant to endure. This can be particularly painful if you're in a monogamous relationship.

In a monogamous relationship. You've been with your lover for five years. You love her dearly, but your sex life just isn't what it used to be. Then you meet another woman, and boom, you're in crush. You feel more sexual passion sitting next to her than you do making love with your partner. Now what do you do?

That's a tough question. Many women have acted on their mad crushes and destroyed solid long-term relationships. If they had it to do over again, they say, they'd do it differently. But, at the time, they felt that they must have the other woman or *die.*

If you decide not to act on your crush, that decision must be followed with action. Work on making sex more exciting with your lover. Avoid spending time alone with the woman on whom you have the crush. And be careful whom you confide your feelings to, since other people's responses can exacerbate your feelings; also, if your confidante tells your lover that you're attracted to someone else, it may hurt your relationship.

On the other hand, some couples are not threatened by each other's crushes, as long as they are confident that their relationship is secure. (There are also couples, in open relationships, whose commitment does not preclude having sex with other women, but most lesbians choose not to handle the stresses of nonmonogamy.)

If you decide to act on your crush, decide first if you're trying to avoid intimacy in your relationship or to fix some unrelated emotional problems. Don't fool yourself that your lover will understand; she probably won't. And if your crush is really a sign that you want out of your relationship, it is simpler and cleaner to break up with your current lover before seeking a new one.

So, here you are with your crush. Do you ignore it? Do you act on it? Or do you just enjoy the little oomph you get when you see her — and then go home to the woman you love?

CRYING. Crying occurs not infrequently in lesbian sex. There are many reasons a woman might cry, ranging from overcoming past abuse to the sheer emotional beauty of making love. Some lesbians cry because for years they feared that they would never get to touch another woman. Lesbian sex can be a miracle, and crying and miracles go together well.

If the woman you are with cries, simply hold her and love her. If you cry, expect the same. If the woman you are with does not support your right to cry, get a new lover.

CUDDLING. True, some women don't enjoy it — nothing on earth pleases *everyone* — but for most lesbians, cuddling ranks up there with sex and breathing.

Cuddling can be foreplay, afterplay, or just its own delight. Cuddling after work helps you leave the day's stress behind; cuddling while watching TV makes any show better; cuddling and chatting is delightful. For many women, an extra thrill of cuddling with another woman is that it doesn't have to lead to sex; in their experiences with men, they couldn't get a hug without being expected to have intercourse.

But while most women love cuddling, many have had to learn to relax and enjoy it. Suzanne says, "I used to need to get away after

making love. I think it had to do some with being raped and some with years and years and years of being a mother and wife and having little space. This relationship is the first where I yearn for skin contact and for being close. When we make love in the afternoon, we'll fall asleep for just ten or fifteen minutes, all wrapped up together, and I love that. One of my favorite ways to cuddle is with her turned over with her back to me, and I put one arm over her and she grabs my hand and my other hand is on her breast and we're touching each other all over."

If you want to cuddle more but are uncomfortable, perhaps as a result of past abuse, let your partner know exactly what works for you. Kathy says, "If I've been having nightmares, the only way I can cuddle is spoons with me behind her. That way I feel safe." Tell your partner what positions you enjoy and find out what her preferences are as well. If you're uncomfortable about your body, her reassurance that she finds you attractive can help you relax. For women who grew up in nonphysical families, learning to enjoy cuddling may take practice. But, oh, are the benefits worth the work! (See also *Sleeping Together; Spoons.*)

CULTURAL DIFFERENCES. Few people growing up in the hyper-race-aware U.S.A. can ignore cultural differences, so intercultural relationships bring unique difficulties. Even if you and she are totally comfortable together, you still have to deal with other people's responses. As Suzanne says, reflecting on a past relationship with a woman of color, "We were breaking a double taboo — you're supposed to be of the same race and different sexes, and we were the opposite!" Unfortunately, some lesbians are no more supportive than heterosexuals around issues of race; all sorts of bigotry are alive and well in the gay community.

The first step in successfully crossing cultural and racial barriers is to let go of attitudes and assumptions. White Anglo-Saxon Protestant women resent being considered cold-blooded and nonsexual every bit as much as ethnic women resent being considered hot-blooded sex machines. Pay attention to who the individual is.

Oppression contests don't help anyone. Kathy says, "I once saw a Jewish woman and a black woman arguing whether the Holocaust was worse than slavery. Can't we just agree that both were terrible beyond measure?"

Denying the importance of a person's background doesn't accomplish anything either. The old cliche of "not noticing" that someone is African-American or Jewish negates the truth that being African-American or Jewish (or poor or rich or Asian-American or Native American or whatever) helps define a person's life and personality.

The trick is to acknowledge the importance of background while respecting people's individuality. A poor white person may have more in common with a poor black person than with a rich white person. Growing up Asian-American in the Southeast of the United States differs significantly from growing up Asian-American in the Northeast. Being an only child in a Native American family differs significantly from being the youngest of five. With all the variations possible, the only way to learn about an individual is to pay careful attention to that individual!

Some people have debated whether it is racist to find only women of a particular race attractive. If a white lesbian always dates black women, is that racism? If a black woman has a thing for Asian-American women, is that racism?

It's impossible to totally unravel the reasons why one person loves or wants another. While striving to end prejudice is an important goal, people love and want the people they love and want. Period. If you love someone and want to be with her and she wants to be with you, it doesn't matter whether you are from identical or different backgrounds. Who you sleep with and who you love are nobody's business but your own. (See also *Types.)*

CUNNILINGUS. See *Oral Sex.*

D

DANCING. Dancing holds a special place in many lesbians' lives, combining fun, an aerobic workout, a chance to meet people, and, sometimes, foreplay or vertical sex.

Lesbian bars may specialize in rock, punk, disco, or country and western, or they may feature different types of music on different nights. Some bars offer dance classes, which are a great way to meet people.

Not all lesbian dancing occurs at bars; in some cities, there are also lesbian dances at gay centers or rented halls. Many women prefer these dances over the bars for their nonalcoholic, nonsmoking environments. In addition, there is the private dancing that a couple may share at home.

Kathy's favorite part of dances is being surrounded by women: "At the first all-women's dance I went to, I was blown away. It was thrilling to see women everywhere, shaking their bodies and grinning ear to ear. What an evening!"

DATING. A famous lesbian joke: What does a lesbian bring on a second date? A U-Haul.

Lesbian romantic interactions tend to cluster into two groups: one-night stands and marriage. It's not surprising, really. Lesbians often come out with a strong sense of time lost, and the last thing we want to do is "waste" more time dating. Whether coming out in our forties after long marriages or in our early twenties having never slept with a man, emerging lesbians don't want to go to the movies and hold hands. We want sex, love, and commitment.

However, dating has much to offer. You can get to know someone gradually, as her personality unfolds over time. Early dates can be activity-oriented, as you go to the movies, play miniature golf, or take walks together. Although many people spill their life stories as soon as they meet, early dating can hold off the emotional and lean toward the friendly. The benefits are enormous, as you take the time to have fun together and discover whether you actually like each other, how much you have in common, how your values match, and other important pieces of information.

Kathy is grateful she finally discovered dating in her thirties: "There was this woman I met who was very attractive. In my old habits, I would have married her within forty-eight hours. Through dating, I discovered that we were not remotely suited to each other. By taking a few weekends to get to know her, I saved myself from a year or two in a disastrous relationship."

Dating can include sex, but sex changes the rules. Expectations heighten. Casualness disappears. As a result, the benefits of dating and slowly getting to know someone may be lessened once you start having sex together.

DENTAL DAMS. See *Safer Sex.*

DIGITAL SEX. See *Fingers; Penetration.*

DILDOS AND BUTT PLUGS. (Objects used for vaginal or anal penetration.)

Once upon a time, mainstream conventional wisdom presumed that all lesbians used dildos; without a penis, went the logic, how could sex happen? However, after the so-called sexual revolution, advanced thinking dismissed this myth as old-fashioned and asserted that lesbians do *not* use dildos.

Guess what? Some lesbians use dildos, and some lesbians don't. Some use them frequently and some use them rarely. Some use them vaginally and some use them anally (i.e., butt plugs) — and some use them both places at the same time.

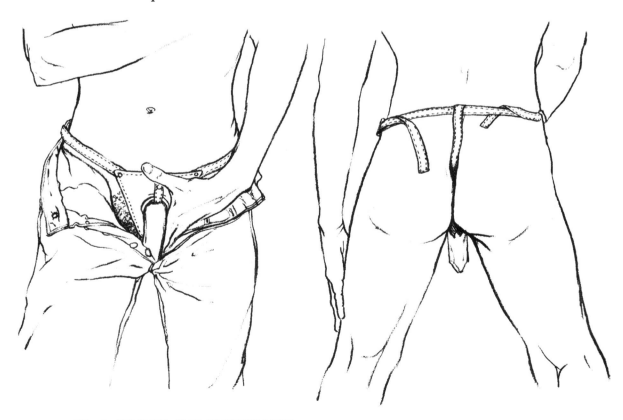

Dictionaries still call dildos "penis substitutes," but in lesbian sex they may be "finger substitutes" — or just their own sweet selves, substituting for nothing.

The world of dildos has changed in the United States in the past twenty years, and a large variety of types is now available. Silicone dildos offer more pliability than plastic, with a softer consistency and a wide assortment of colors (lavender is particularly popular with lesbians); dildos also come in many shapes, including corncobs, fists, dolphins, and the very lesbian fingers model. Some have doo-dads attached to stimulate the clitoris during penetration; some are two-ended to penetrate two women at the same time. The sizes available range from tiny to humongous.

Choosing the dildo. If your neighborhood lacks an "adult bookstore" or some other place where you can purchase a dildo, or if only a limited selection is available, see *Mail Order.* There are so many sorts of dildos out there that it's worth searching for exactly the one you want.

Choosing the right dildo size may be trickier than it seems. You can make a preliminary decision based on how many fingers you find comfortable inside you, but that may not be large enough; it's easier to take in a smooth dildo than knuckled fingers. Basing dildo size on sexual experience with men can also be misleading. When Alice started having sex with women, she discovered that, although her last male lover had been quite large, she actually preferred penetration with a smaller dildo. With men, she was stuck with the penis that came attached, but with women, she enjoyed her freedom of choice. (To experiment with different dildo sizes without spending a fortune, see *Vegetables.)*

You will also have to decide what material dildo you prefer. Do you want a rigid dildo? Then go for plastic. For a more giving feel, try silicone. Note, however, that silicone is damaged more easily than plastic.

For shape and color, just pick what amuses you and turns you on. While some women prefer non-penis-shaped dildos, others find the old standard to be sexier. To each her own.

For anal use, butt plugs offer many advantages over plastic or silicone dildos. They are firmer and often smaller, with a tapered shape to facilitate insertion. Widened ends keep the butt plug from slipping all the way in the butt.

Hygiene. If your dildo has any breaks on its surface, always use a condom with it; those breaks will make it difficult to keep the dildo clean. In addition, use condoms when sharing dildos with other women to avoid also sharing vaginal infections. Long-term couples often have two (or more) dildos so that each partner can choose her own size, color, and shape; these separate dildos also help keep the occasional yeast infection from going back and forth from one lover to the other.

An item that has been used anally should not be used vaginally. If only one dildo is available, using a condom for anal use and then a new condom for vaginal use should afford protection from infection, but it's safer to have different items for each location. If you can only afford one dildo, consider using a butt plug for anal penetration and investigating cucumbers and other vegetables for vaginal penetration.

After every use, wash the dildo or butt plug thoroughly with warm soap and water.

Using the dildo. Vaginal penetration with a dildo can occur by hand or using a harness to attach it at the crotch. A fun approach is to put the harness on under 501 jeans, open one button, and have the dildo stick through.

To start with, make sure the dildo is well lubricated. Even if your lover is extremely wet, additional lubrication makes penetration more comfortable: the bigger the dildo, the more lubrication is needed.

Unless your partner craves instant vigorous penetration, enter her slowly and gracefully. Once inside, stay still for a while so that her vagina can become accustomed to the size of the dildo.

Wielding a strapped-on dildo takes skill and stamina. Until you've acquired those, a sense of humor will come in handy. Leave time for experimentation and silliness when you first try strapping one on.

Positions. The following positions are described from the point of view of the woman wearing the harness and dildo. (With the hand-held dildo, almost any position is possible.)

In the legendary missionary position, your partner lies on her back, legs spread, and you lie on her, your legs between hers. Either of you can guide the dildo into her. She wraps her legs around your back or bends her knees with her feet on the bed. Thrust from your hips or from your thighs or sort of bounce up and down. To increase your stamina, alternate approaches so that one muscle group can rest while another does the work. If you are both thrusting, it may take a while to coordinate your rhythms; to the extent you physically can, follow her lead.

In an option for the very limber, she brings her knees to her chest with her feet next to her head. This position facilitates particularly deep penetration.

In some positions, the dildo wearer is on the bottom, as in the reversed missionary position. Or you lie on your back on the bed and then she sits down on the dildo, either facing you or with her back to you. In this position, you flex your buttocks or sway your hips from side to side to thrust, or she bounces up and down, or you use a combination of strategies. She may masturbate as well.

Many women enjoy being entered "doggie style." She gets on her hands and knees, and you kneel behind her, then enter her. (She may prefer to kneel on the floor and lean on the bed, a chair, or a table.) This position has many advantages. Rear entry facilitates aiming the dildo at her G-spot, and neither of you has to lean on the other, so fewer limbs fall asleep. In addition, she can easily reach her clitoris if she desires. And holding a woman by her hips as you penetrate her from behind is very sexy.

Penetration can also occur with the two of you lying on your sides, face-to-face or one behind the other. Face-to-face is more difficult to pull off, as your legs may get in each other's way.

Some women can have orgasms from being penetrated; others can't. Some like hard fucking; others like long graceful strokes. Some like penetration to last forever; others consider a few minutes sufficient. Preferences may vary depending on mood, menstrual cycle, and amount of arousal. If you're not sure whether she likes what you're doing, ask! (Similarly, if you're being penetrated, let her know what you want.)

For a unique experience, go down on your lover while she has a dildo strapped on. That is, lick and suck the dildo. This might happen before she has penetrated you or afterward, when you will be licking your own juices off of "her." If the idea doesn't gross you out or bother your politics, try it. Many women find it hot! (But *never* put anything in your mouth that has been in an anus.)

Some women wear dildos under their clothing to go out dancing. When they rub against a partner, she may be shocked — or thrilled.

If you just don't enjoy dildos, don't worry. As Rebecca says, "A finger has much more flexibility and intelligence than a piece of plastic." (See also *Penetration.*)

DISABILITIES. Since disabilities vary from chronic back pain to quadriplegia, from deafness to blindness, from lost limbs to cancer, and since individual women respond to their disabilities in individual ways, there is no magic formula that people with disabilities and their lovers can follow to have great sex. However, there are useful guidelines.

First of all, honest and explicit communication between the partners is imperative. While the partner with the disability will need to educate her lover as to her sexual abilities, limitations, desires, and fears, the nondisabled partner needs also to express *her* desires and fears. Conversations can be a sort of foreplay; one woman may lead the other on a tour of those parts of her body she enjoys having touched.

In addition, discuss vocabulary preferences. While some lesbians insist on the phrase "people who are physically challenged,"

others prefer "people with disabilities." Some have reclaimed "cripples" or "crips" in much the same way some lesbians and gay men have reclaimed "queer." Words influence how we think and how we perceive each other, and conversations will flow more smoothly with an agreed-upon vocabulary.

Remember that the woman with the disability does not "limit the sex life." The *disability* does. And no one must deal with any limitations more directly than the woman does. This is particularly important to remember when a woman has invisible disabilities. Alice says, "When I was with Lisa, who had limited energy because of health problems, I got angry when she chose to expend that energy on work, say, or dancing, rather than sex. It took me too long to recognize that the priority was hers to set."

Jessica, who tires easily because of an immune system disorder, explains, "It's been tough when I've been with someone who's very active and not willing to make the effort to understand that I just don't have a lot of energy."

Rebecca, who has heart problems, says, "With lovers who were healthy, everything about the relationship, including sex, was too tiring. And it was hard for me to say no. I guess I was embarrassed to say, 'Gee, I really don't feel well.'"

Both Jessica and Rebecca are now involved with women who also have disabilities. "I'm very happy to have a lover who also has an illness," Rebecca explains. "If I want to make love, and I see that she's tired, I wouldn't even consider pushing it. Or if I'm tired, she doesn't push. We just understand that about each other. The pace is much better."

Jessica says that people don't understand why she's with her lover, who is quite ill: "Some people say, 'Why do you fall in love with women with serious illnesses?' Well, I have a serious illness — do they mean it's not okay to fall in love with me?"

It's clear that some nondisabled women seriously need to have their consciousnesses raised about women with disabilities and disability issues. *With the Power of Each Breath: A Disabled Women's Anthology* has 350 pages of stories, essays, poetry, interviews, and letters describing the experiences of women with disabilities. In addition, *Sapphistry* discusses various disabilities and their effects on sex one by one, with useful advice on how to work around sexual limitations and enhance sexual pleasure. (See also *Mastectomy.*)

DISCIPLINE. See *Sadomasochism.*

DOCTORS. See *Health.*

DOUCHING. See *Cleanliness.*

DRUGS. If you use illegal drugs, keep in mind that, in some states, "no-tolerance" laws put social drug users behind bars for longer than murderers. In a recent case, someone was sentenced to fifteen years in jail for possession of a small amount of LSD; it seems the weight of the paper to which the drug was attached topped some arbitrary limit! Be familiar with your state's laws before you take a chance.

That being said, it is also true that many people find that occasional drug use enhances their sex lives. (See also *Alcohol and Drug Use.*)

E

EARS. Do not underestimate the sensitivity of ears! Inside and out, ears can provide thrills down the neck, throughout the body, to the toes.

Nibble her lobe. Breathe and whisper sweet things, or sweet nothings. Outline her ear with your tongue, then penetrate it gently.

Always be careful; ears are tender places, and eardrums are not replaceable. Also, monitor your lover's responses. If she has sensitive ears, she will adore what you are doing, but it's possible that ear stimulation will do nothing for her — or will even annoy her. If you're not sure of her reaction, a breathy, warm, whispered, "Do you like this?" into her ear should get you a useful response.

EJACULATION. See *G-Spot.*

EMOTIONS. Sex carries with it the baggage of social myths and childhood training. One particularly onerous piece of luggage preaches that sex and love travel hand in hand in a simple, unbreakable tandem. In truth, some sex is emotional; some isn't. Sex may be emotional for one partner and not the other. Or sex may throb with emotion, but that emotion may not be love.

Where the myth and the truth meet is a dangerous intersection. For instance, if a woman experiences incredibly exciting sex with someone, she may instantly believe that partner is the love of her life. After all, "good sex equals true love," right? However, days, weeks, or even years down the line, she may realize she doesn't love, or even *like,* the partner at all; she only enjoys the sex.

Even with a partner you love and like, you will not both experience the same emotions at the same time during sex or daily life. If you have a great encounter and she doesn't, that doesn't make either of you wrong. Nor were your feelings false. Maybe you always experience peak emotions during sex, but she focuses on the physical. Maybe she needs to be distant from her emotions in order to be sexual, as may happen in incest survivors. Are you two incompatible? Not necessarily. If you love each other, or just really want to have sex, you can simply accept that you are together in different ways, but still together. Give each other room to be emotional or distant. If necessary, take turns having your emotional needs met as you would take turns having your physical needs met. Most importantly, remember that there are no rules about when to feel a certain way, and anyone who tries to force such rules on you is wrong.

The ideal that making love should consist of two people reaching higher and higher levels of mutual ecstasy and closeness, all the while feeling deeper and deeper love, is just that: an ideal. If it happens, thank your lucky stars. But to seek that mutuality as a constant goal is destructive, particularly in a community where so many women have suffered some form of sexual abuse in their past. (See also *Crying; Laughter.)*

EROTICA. See *Pornography.*

EXHIBITIONISM. (The public flaunting of one's body or genitals.)

Isn't it odd that, in a world where people at the beach wear the skimpiest of bathing suits and Cher and Madonna are superstars, public nudity is illegal? But it is, and in most locations, behavior that a straight couple might get away with, a lesbian couple won't. As a result, lesbian public displays mostly occur in two venues: gay pride marches, where many Dykes on Bikes go topless, and women's music festivals, where virtually *everyone* goes topless. There's safety in numbers.

Private exhibitionism is another story entirely. Many women enjoy making love with a partner in front of a mirror; others enjoy strip-teases or dancing nude. Masturbating while a partner watches can enhance the experience for both women, and part of the thrill of group sex is having so many people look on.

Since the word *exhibitionism* carries the connotation of a sleazy guy in a raincoat displaying his wares to passersby, perhaps there needs to be a new word for, shall we say, vanilla exhibitionism. How about "showing off" or "private performance"? Whatever the term, the experience can be loads of fun.

EX-LOVERS. It is not unusual for a lesbian's ex-lover to be her best friend. Of course, it is also not unusual for a lesbian's ex-lover to be her worst enemy, but, due to the smallness of most lesbian communities, there is often pressure for exes to get along.

Alice says, "When my ex and I broke up, she got custody of the bars and I got custody of the Friday night support group. We occasionally bumped into each other at dances, though, and that was terrible. Years later, I still hate seeing her unexpectedly." Yet Alice has been close friends with another ex for years.

When asked how long it takes to be able to deal with an ex-lover, Rebecca replied, "Oh, two or three more lovers."

Sometimes, after a breakup, your ex-lover may start to look incredibly sexy to you, and you'll be tempted to sleep with her again. One last time. No strings attached. For old time's sake. A rematch of this sort will often be the best sex you two have had in years. However, while many women make a smooth transition from being lovers to being friends who occasionally have sex, others sleep with their exes one or two times and then decide it's too heartbreaking. Still others wouldn't make love with an ex for a million dollars.

How any two women deal with each other after a breakup depends entirely on their specific needs. Although it may seem easier to remain in touch, particularly in a small community, sometimes a clean break works better. Kathy says, "I used to be proud that I remained friendly with my exes; it seemed so very dyky. Now I find it easier to just move on."

Whatever road you take in dealing with your ex-lover, the book *Unbroken Ties: Lesbian Ex-Lovers* may be of help to you.

Then there's the challenge of being in a relationship with a woman whose most recent ex-lover is her best friend! (See also *Jealousy.*)

EXPECTATIONS. Growing up in a society that is simultaneously sex-obsessed and sex-phobic can lead to unrealistic sexual expectations, since sex is both overrated and underrated. Movies present images of passion so strong that people's brains melt to mud, while religious fundamentalists attack nonheterosexual, nonmarital sex as evil, ignoring its potential beauty, spirituality, and bonding power.

In real life, sex is many things to many people, and occasionally it is disappointing. Anyone expecting a smooth, passionate, transcendent experience every single time she makes love will get her heart broken in short order. Sex can be inept, boring, and awkward.

It can also be stunningly moving and life-changing.

The best expectations to have are as few as possible. Be ready to enjoy whatever happens; that will bring you more pleasure than awaiting a fantasy that never quite arrives. Expecting fireworks can make you miss the wind in the trees.

Rebecca says, "I've become a lot more reasonable about my expectations. I used to expect to be totally seduced, swept off my feet. The earth was supposed to shake every single time I made love. And the first time that didn't happen, I'd think, well, it's time to leave this person. Now I have an overview. There're different kinds of sex. There's lazy sex, there's sex that you just have in a comfortable nice way, there's sex for release of tension, and sometimes there's very exciting sex. I don't expect that tremendous excitement all the time anymore. And I'm really very grateful for the pleasure that my lover gives me."

Expectations pose even more dangers in relationships. Too often, partners who experience great sex together anticipate that they will always get along in every way, every day, all the time. But it never turns out like that. Real relationships, with their ups and downs and ebbs and flows, cannot hold a candle to dearly held expectations of flawlessness, so too many couples abandon good relationships to search for perfection — and all are disappointed in their quests.

Life is full of surprises, some of them terrible. But some surprises surpass anyone's imagination; why allow expectations to get in the way?

F

FANTASIES. Some women are embarrassed by their sexual fantasies, while others adore theirs. It's not a matter of content; one woman may be uncomfortable at fantasizing vanilla sex with two strangers or a rock star, while another may feel great imagining an S/M orgy with an entire rugby team.

There are two basic and conflicting truths about sexual fantasies: (1) All fantasies are fine, since they exist only in the imagination, where no damage is done and where no one else need ever find out. (2) Many women, particularly those whose fantasies reflect abuse they suffered as children, hate the stories that their heads tell them during sex.

Women who do not enjoy their fantasies can train themselves either to change or to accept those fantasies. JoAnn Loulan suggests in *Lesbian Sex* that you alter just one small feature of your fantasy at a time, be it the person, the location, the position, or whatever.

To take the other road and accept your fantasies, remind yourself, over and over again if necessary, "This is okay, this is okay." Reading about what other women fantasize may also help, particularly when you discover that what goes on in your head isn't unusual at all.

What *do* other women fantasize? Let's hear from the interviewees.

Gail says she fantasizes "all the time. A lot of times I fantasize about scenes that I've seen in adult films. Usually they're het oriented — meaning I see a male and a female. Or I fantasize about a sexual act that I've been a part of and I just relive that moment."

Lydia says, "My fantasies move further on as I do. I have a couple of favorite fantasies now — real solid favorites. One is being seduced by a really butch top in the back of a limousine, and the other one is being taken by a gang of rather butch S/M tops — kind of like the *Macho Sluts* story, which is one of my favorites. I have fashions and fads in fantasies. I'll go with one or two for a long time."

Jessica says she has managed to live out many of her fantasies, but she still occasionally fantasizes "about men having sex together. I've done that since I was a kid. And sometimes I'll fantasize about a man making love to a woman, but that woman won't necessarily be me."

Alice's fantasies include movie stars: "I've had sex with Linda Hamilton, Sigourney Weaver, and Marlene Dietrich."

Suzanne's fantasies run quite a large gamut: "I've had containment or rape fantasies. Penetration fantasies. Being held down, tied down, strapped down, and, very often, by something mechanical — no people, which I think was nice for a while. Not threatening. When I was first coming out, I fantasized that men were tied up watching me. They'd be tied up or chained against a wall and watching me with a woman or several women making love to me. And they were just going nuts. That was kind of neat. It was a revenge fantasy at the same time it was a sexual fantasy. I have brief fantasies about penises, but without the rest that goes with them. A dildo is just fine, because I'm just not interested in hairy hard bodies. One fantasy sort of creature that I have in my head is an androgyne hermaphrodite with a wonderful penetrating organ but everything else is pretty much a woman's body — wonderful breasts and voluptuousness and a woman-type muscly figure."

Rebecca has made an uneasy peace with her fantasies: "My fantasies have to do with control; mostly, the women are seduced against their will. I'm pretty sure they're replays of what I saw when I was a child, and they're upsetting to me. I don't like having them. People need to do things to get off, but I don't go along with the school of thought that says it's great — although I have finally accepted that I have to allow myself that in order to enjoy sex. If that's the way I've been damaged, I'm not going to damage myself further by killing my sex life. I guess everybody has to set their own limits. It isn't feminist and wonderful, but I'm going to allow myself to enjoy it."

Jenn's experience has been quite different: "Basically, I get to live out my fantasies. Whenever my lover or I ever want anything, we discuss it and try it."

When do women have fantasies? All sorts of times: during masturbation, during sex, standing on line at the grocery store, riding the bus, at work, and at the movies. Or only during masturbation. Or only during sex. Or never.

If you want to extend your fantasy repertoire, see *Pornography*.

FEMALE EJACULATION. See *G-Spot*.

FEMINISM. If *feminism* is defined as "loving and supporting women and working toward our achieving a full and equal place in society," then most, if not all, lesbians are feminists. But the word *feminism* has many connotations in the lesbian community, including "a belief in political correctness, with biases against butch/femme roles and S/M sex," "a hatred of men and unwillingness to deal with them," and "radical beliefs in overthrowing society as it exists." Not surprisingly, the last three definitions leave many lesbians feeling distinctly *un*-feminist. In addition, many younger women consider woman-only events and organizations totally outmoded; they ally comfortably with men and even occasionally have sex with them.

Many women who do identify as feminists have ambivalent feelings about the label, particularly when they do not agree with every idea that is supposed to be part of feminism. As S/M practitioner Lydia answered, when asked how her feminism affects her sex life, "I try not to let it. Obviously, I don't toe the politically correct line that some people have of what is proper sexual behavior for the correct dyke. And I don't feel any guilt or confusion about that. Which occasionally confuses me." Lydia says that, overall, feminism has affected her positively: "It has given me a better sense of myself and more of a willingness to be truthful and adventurous."

The other women interviewed for this book, all of whom identify as feminists, feel largely positive about their beliefs. Rebecca says that feminism has helped her with honesty in sex, and adds, "Sex with a woman is a revolutionary act, and that is a dimension that I love."

But lesbians are not required to be feminists, just as lesbians are not required to be Democrats, TV watchers, dancers, or bodybuilders. Nor are lesbian feminists required to have sex a certain way, fantasize a certain way, or have relationships a certain way. (See also *Political Correctness.*)

FINDING A LOVER. See *Meeting People.*

FINGERS. Fingers own a place of honor in lesbian sexuality. Suzanne says, "Definitely, hands are something I notice. Breasts are lovely, but hands are the things that turn me on."

This is not to say there is one model of the "sexy lesbian hand." While many women agree with Suzanne that "long and flexible fingers are exciting," a lover of Jessica's appreciated that Jessica's entire small hand could fit inside her. Still other women don't pay much attention to hands, particularly women who aren't into penetration.

But there are certain traits that lesbian hand-cruisers all appreciate in hands, such as cleanliness and short, smoothly filed nails. No one wants to be stabbed internally. (See also *Penetration.*)

FIRST LOVE. Lesbian first love can be heartbreaking, as it often isn't consummated. Because so many lesbians discover their homosexuality before we know other lesbians, we often fall in love with straight women. Kathy says, "When I fell in love with my best friend, I didn't even understand what was going on. She had to tell me, and of course she wasn't interested in me that way. It was all very painful."

Sadly enough, one's first crush on another lesbian offers no consummation guarantees either. Alice relates, "When I finally came out, and I finally met other lesbians, and I finally got a crush on one and I finally had the nerve to ask her out, I was astonished when she said no! I thought I was finished with the hard part."

Even when a lesbian does get to sleep with her first love, "happily ever after" often proves elusive. Many lesbians spend their adolescence stuck in a closet and unable to date the people they want to date, thus missing the chance to learn basic relationship skills. It's difficult to come out with adult needs and emotions but teenage expectations and desires. As a result, many lesbians handle their first love affairs awkwardly or downright badly.

Of course, some women knew as teens that they were gay and managed same-sex teen relationships, but their first loves, too, often ended sadly, as the lover decided she was straight or their parents found out and forbade them to see each other.

This may seem a dour way to discuss first love, but, unfortunately, the sweet and tender first-love experience is one of the things homophobia often steals from lesbians. Oppression does take its toll. However, as lesbians come out, learn to deal with homophobia (internal and external), acquire some romantic experience, and grow up, we can gain all the skills we need for healthy relationships and find lesbians who love us and treat us well. Even when first love hurts, second or third love can be glorious.

And times are changing. As women recognize their homosexuality earlier — and accept themselves earlier — they can be happy earlier. Kathy knows a long-term couple, sane and quite in love, who met years ago in college; neither has ever been involved with anyone else. Their first loves are each other, and their relationship is a total success. (See also *Dating.*)

THE FIRST TIME.

The first time having lesbian sex. The First Time having lesbian sex can be terrifying or wonderful. Frequently it is both. Some women have enjoyed a First Time with someone they didn't know well, but they probably constitute a minority. For most women, it's worth waiting for someone you can trust to care about you — not necessarily forever, but at least for the First Time.

Kathy recalls her first female lover: "I had sex with men only to prove I was 'normal,' so I wasn't that careful about who I slept with. When I started to come out, I decided to be more choosy. I waited until I met a lovely, sweet, considerate dyke who was pleased to make love to me. Waiting was a wonderful gift to myself, even though we didn't end up in a relationship."

This does not connote a lesbianized version of "Waiting for Ms. Right." Rather, taking time so that you can feel safe and comfortable during one of the most important experiences of your life is, as Kathy says, a gift to yourself. A bad initial experience may echo throughout your future sex life, while a fun and affectionate First Time can ready you for a fun and affectionate second time — and third time. And if you seek emotional, deep, and spiritual sex, take particular care in choosing your first lover.

Of course, having sex with a woman does not instantly clear up coming-out issues. Use the period before (and after) your First Time to read, go to support groups, make new friends, and discover where you fit in the lesbian community.

Many women experience a sense of wonder or relief the First Time they actually get to touch another woman. Suzanne says, "I remember being amazed that, *this is happening*, it's really happening and I'm not being struck dead. I was amazed how normal it felt. I'd been thinking about it so damn long."

Unfortunately, tyro dykes face a prevalent prejudice in the lesbian community. This bias results from numerous experienced lesbians having been left by numerous neophytes, as the rookies panic, return to the closet, or simply move on. This prejudice is unfair, since plenty of lesbians have also been left by *experienced* lesbians, but it does exist.

However, don't succumb to the temptation to exaggerate your experience; that approach often backfires. If a potential lover won't accept you as you are, who needs her? Keep looking. There are millions of lesbians out there! Suzanne defied conventional wisdom and took a chance with a newly out woman, and three years later, they're both still thrilled that she did.

The first time having sex with a particular woman. Even if you are an experienced lesbian, you may still feel nervous the first time you have sex with a particular woman. You may fear not pleasing her; you may worry that she won't like your body. Keep in mind, however, that she is going to bed with you *because* you please her and she likes your body.

If she makes love to you first, pay attention to how she does it; women often touch their partners as they'd like to be touched themselves. (If she's recently out of a relationship, however, she may touch you the way her ex-lover liked to be touched!)

When you make love to her, remember that sex is not a mind-reading test. If the two of you jump into bed tearing off each other's clothes and everything feels perfect, congratulations. However, it's also okay to simply ask her what she likes. Your attention and concern will probably delight her. It's even okay to admit you're scared, if indeed you are. Just keep the tone sexy, and you can turn information exchange into verbal foreplay.

As much as you want to please her, don't strut all your stuff the first time around; save some surprises for later. (See also *Communication.*)

FISTING. (Penetrating a woman's vagina with your entire hand; also known as fist-fucking.)

First it's important to talk about what fisting isn't. Fisting isn't pushing your already-folded-up hand into a woman. Nor is it particularly kinky. Some women have given birth to large children, and, as Suzanne says, "My biggest kid was 9 pounds, 3 ounces, and that's bigger than a woman's hand!" Some women who have not given birth just have naturally large capacities, and still others are turned on by being full, full, full. Suzanne adds, "I think it's something that needs to be taken out of the realm of strange, 'cause it really is quite nice and quite lovely."

Techniques. If your lover is experienced in being fisted and requests that you do so, ask what she likes, and listen carefully to her response. Fisting is a delicate and exact science. Don't even attempt it if either of you is drunk or stoned. File your nails short and smooth or use a latex glove (not a powdered glove, which dries up lubrication). Take off any rings and bracelets. *Use plenty of lubricant.*

If you and your lover are feeling your way through a first-time attempt at fisting, start by inserting one or two fingers. As your lover's arousal level grows, add another finger and then another. Using a palm-up angle, as your hand goes further and deeper inside her, add your thumb across your palm. Then, following the contours of her vagina, gently fold your four fingers over your thumb into a fist. With this motion, slip the rest of your hand in. Voila!

Experiment with different movements. Use a gentle in-and-out motion without actually removing your hand, or twirl your hand back and forth inside her. Try opening and closing your fingers so that they touch, tap, or massage her vagina's upper walls. With a little aim and practice, that motion can stimulate her G-spot, leading to some serious ecstasy.

Once you've ascertained what she likes, more vigorous movement may be in order. Then again, it may not. If you're unsure what she wants, ask her.

Once she has reached orgasm or signaled that she wants you to come out of her, gently start slipping your hand out, unfolding your fingers as you do so. If you feel stuck, ask her to lead you out. If you feel that your hand has been suctioned in, open her vagina a little wider with your other hand to break the vacuum.

While fisting requires that you focus on her responses, you may be stunned at your own. Being enveloped in a hot, throbbing vagina is heavenly.

Read "A Hand in the Bush" and "Fisting Two" in *Susie Sexpert's Lesbian Sex World* for downright inspiring discussions of fisting.

FOOD. Food is the lesbian blessing and the lesbian curse. While many women associate eating with sensuality and incorporate meals into their foreplay, others battle bulimia and anorexia. Because of discomfort with their weight, even women without eating disorders often limit what they eat, yet they still relish good food — and may use edibles as sex toys.

Alice finds Japanese food a turn-on and says, "Sushi is the next best thing to eating pussy." Suzanne finds that "food is good foreplay — a nice dinner, with artichokes and things like that." Jenn enjoyed the time she licked whipped cream off her lover's body, and Gail likes to incorporate ice and honey (not at the same time!) into oral sex. However, Kathy says, "Honey is just too messy to be fun."

Many lesbians are vegetarians, so don't invite her to a steak house on your first date.

FOREPLAY. Where does lesbian foreplay end and sex begin? Does it matter?

Suzanne's comments on foreplay reflect the feelings of many lesbians: "I almost want to laugh when you talk about foreplay between women, because, with men, foreplay was all the stuff I liked — which they would do a little bit of on the way to what *they* liked. Even clitoris was foreplay, which just seems bizarre to me! With women, foreplay never stops. That old 'first base, second base' stuff seems to not have any meaning with women."

Nevertheless, many women still prefer that making love begin with extensive nongenital activity. Rebecca says, "I have fears around sex, and I need a lot of holding and hugging and kissing and loving. I need to feel turned on and also very safe."

Foreplay can include cuddling, kissing, stroking, and massage. Sweet conversation can be foreplay, as can a nice walk together.

Of course, there are also times when both partners *aren't* in the mood for foreplay and jump right into oral sex or penetration. There's no magic formula of 30 percent kissing, 15 percent stroking, 10 percent humping, 20 percent licking, 20 percent penetration, and 5 percent sweating; every approach can be exciting and wonderful.

FREQUENCY. There is no Official Correct Frequency for having or wanting sex. Rebecca prefers an intense weekend of sex once a month, while Suzanne craves a regular diet of twice-weekly lovemaking.

Women's desires may vary depending on the time of month and their energy levels, physical health, other commitments, psychological health, and whether or not they're in love. Early in relationships, many women can't keep their hands off each other, while a year or two later, having sex once a week will be just fine. Yet five or ten years down the road, some couples start having sex all the time again.

Rebecca comments, "To me the important thing is not how often I have sex — it's that I should enjoy sex when I have it."

All frequency desires are fine, in and of themselves. But what happens when a couple's preferences don't match? The first thing to remember is that no one is right and no one is wrong. She's not a sex maniac, and you're not frigid — nor vice versa.

Examine why one woman has different desires than the other. Is one working harder? Dealing with molestation issues? Having health problems? Or is she responding to problems she perceives in the relationship?

Don't assume that the person working harder or dealing with molestation issues is the one who wants *less* sex. People respond to different pressures in different ways.

Talking may solve the frequency-difference problem all by itself, particularly if the partners simply need reassurance that they are loved. Once the couple feel secure, they can negotiate a compromise to meet both their needs. For instance, they may agree to have sex more often during vacations or decide to have sex dates once a week.

Unfortunately, sometimes these problems are more serious, particularly if one partner really wants to leave the relationship. Or a couple may love each other a lot, but just have wildly different sexual desire levels. If the couple can't work it out, therapy may help, whether to find a new way to go on or to end the relationship gracefully.

If you and your partner make love unusually often, unusually rarely, or even never, but you both feel that your needs are being met, you have no problem at all. However, consider keeping information about an unusual sexual frequency to yourselves, so that well-meaning and not-so-well-meaning friends don't try to convince you that something is wrong with your relationship.

FUCKING. See *Anal Sex; Fingers; Penetration; Vocabulary.*

G

G-SPOT. The section *Anatomy* includes a description of the G-spot and how to locate it.

G stands for Ernst Grafenberg, the doctor who supposedly "discovered" the G-spot (want to bet how many women already knew about it?). Suzanne complains, "I don't like that it's named after a guy," but Kathy says, "I just think of it as the noise I make when it's touched; you know, *'Gee,* that feels good!'"

Stimulating the G-spot can cause vaginal orgasms, which may be accompanied by ejaculation. Yes, some women do ejaculate. That is, when they come, a clear liquid — not urine — spurts out through the urethra. Because the urethra is the internal tube through which urine leaves the body, because G-spot stimulation makes some women feel like they have to urinate, and because few people had heard of female ejaculation until relatively recently, for years women were mortified when they ejaculated. They thought they were peeing when they came.

That feeling of a need to pee, plus the idea that peeing during sex is embarrassing and horrible, has stopped many women from allowing themselves to reach vaginal orgasm and ejaculate. But, again, *ejaculate is not urine,* and, even if it were, it wouldn't be the end of the world. Kathy says, "One of my ex-lovers peed when she came — or ejaculated, I guess. Anyway, at the time we thought it was pee, but we just always had towels around."

The G-spot first received extensive publicity through the book *The G Spot and Other Recent Discoveries about Human Sexuality,* which briefly mentions lesbians: "Our preliminary findings indicate that there may be a higher incidence of female ejaculation in the lesbian population than there is among heterosexual women." The authors postulated that fingers are more adept for G-spot manipulation than penises.

Not all lesbians have vaginal orgasms, not all lesbians who have vaginal orgasms ejaculate, and not all lesbians enjoy having their G-spot stimulated. Many gay women, including Jenn and Gail, had never heard of female ejaculation until Susie Bright started publicizing it in her sex talks.

Women who want to learn how to have vaginal orgasms and ejaculate often can. After years of sexual experience, Suzanne says, "One of my recent discoveries is 'waterfalls,' — the term 'female ejaculation' is just too ugly. It is a very different sensation, and very powerful. That's the thing that leaves me shuddering hours later."

If you've never had a G-spot orgasm, with or without ejaculation, and you want to, see *Vaginal Orgasms*. For a vivid education in ejaculation, including footage of women actually having G-spot orgasms, check out the video *How to Female Ejaculate*. (See also *Anatomy*; *Orgasms*; *Penetration*.)

GENDER. Once upon a time, gender seemed a simple thing. Men and women knew their places, which were highly defined and very specific. Now, the lines have blurred. Harriet doesn't stay home with the kids while Ozzie goes to work. The heroine doesn't stand around and wait for the hero to rescue her, then sweep her off her feet. In the lesbian community, the lines are even blurrier, leaving each lesbian to express herself as she sees fit, rather than according to mainstream society's guidelines.

Many lesbians have experienced the feeling of being very different from heterosexual women. Kathy tells of standing on line in the bathroom at a Deborah Harry concert: "All the women had tons of makeup and short leather skirts. They looked nothing like dykes. Sometimes I think lesbians are a different gender than straight women. Actually, the only gay people I've ever seen who looked like those women were men!"

In reality, "lipstick lesbians" do look like the women at that concert. Others look like little boys. Others look like stereotypical moms, and still others look like movie stars.

But changing views of gender go past the details of clothing and makeup, as shown by the boomlet among both men and women of transsexual operations. Men become women, women become men, and occasional individuals choose a hermaphroditic body with breasts and a penis. Some transsexuals express themselves heterosexually in their new bodies, some homosexually.

In the past, people who had sex-change operations talked of feeling that they were in the "wrong body"; some later said that they were gay but couldn't accept it. Nowadays, people still have operations to find the "right body," but others change and sculpt their bodies to express themselves.

When transsexuals speak of feeling that they were in the wrong body, they are speaking their truth. Their willingness to undergo painful and expensive operations emphasizes how important that truth is. And, considering that human variation includes children born as hermaphrodites and people with unusual combinations of X and Y chromosomes, transsexuals who say that they were in the wrong body may well be supported by biology.

If you feel that you are in the wrong body and are considering surgery, start by finding a support group. It is unlikely that you will get honest, understanding, and useful information from mainstream therapists or doctors. Lesbian and gay centers often have information on transsexual organizations.

In our society, with its knee-jerk oppression of sexual difference, transsexuals — whether gay or straight, male or female — have much in common with lesbians. While transsexuality may sound shocking, it is worth remembering that anyone who pushes the boundaries of gender restrictions helps all of us. And the boundaries do need constant expanding.

Just thirty years ago in the United States, women were required to wear girdles and skirts; they weren't allowed to be athletic because the powers-that-be feared they would damage their uteruses; the best jobs were closed to women; women couldn't travel alone; and in some cities, women wearing fewer than two pieces of "female clothing" could be arrested. Even today, gender restrictions limit women's career options, with the legendary "glass ceiling" keeping them from many boardrooms and government offices. In addition, only women who follow the gender rules make it far enough to hit that ceiling; try being successful in most professions without putting on a skirt or a dress and hose!

As long as society gets away with deciding that women must dress one way and men another, that only heterosexual sex is acceptable, that men and women differ in personality and skills, gender will remain a jail cell. Lesbians and transsexuals are only two of the groups trying to break free.

GENITALS. Not all lesbians automatically fall madly in love with female genitals — their own or other women's. Many young girls are taught that their "private parts" are dirty and not to be touched; when they grow up, they may need to work hard to overcome that training.

If you are uneasy about female genitals, spend time looking at your vulva in a mirror. Play with your labia. Masturbate and watch the changes your genitals go through. Feel and smell your lubrication. Remember to breathe and relax; it's not a test, it's an exploration. Have fun.

Don't expect to immediately love everything you see and feel and taste. Give yourself time to get over past taboos.

If you have a willing partner, examine her vulva and compare it to your own. See the different ways that labia are shaped and the different colorations. Stroke her and yourself. Discuss what you like and dislike. Getting to know your vulvas better will help you to love them.

Kathy says, "The first time I went down on a woman, I was terrified. She had just gone down on me, so I asked her, mostly to stall for time, 'Are you built like me?' She answered in detail, telling me how my clit was right out there, while hers was more buried under her labia. It helped so much to take a second and talk."

Once you are past the taboos, you may discover that you adore female genitals and love to touch and lick them. When asked about her preferred body parts, Lydia said, "I really like cunts. I like my own and I like other women's. I really like the look, I like the smell, I like the texture, I like the taste. It's my favorite part."

GOOD LOVER. Many newly out lesbians fear being bad lovers. Jessica says, "When I first thought I was going to finally sleep with a woman, I did tongue exercises — I would stick my tongue out and pretend I was licking and watch myself." Jessica was trying to improve both her technique and her stamina. But the myth that a good lover must have the technique of a musician, the sexuality of a movie star, and the stamina of an athlete does not reflect the reality of the women interviewed for this book.

Rebecca prefers "somebody I can really be in contact with — with a real exchange of caring." Gail says, "What turns me on is someone who is responsive, someone who is willing to talk about what she likes and what she wants, someone who is willing to take risks, someone who is comfortable with her body, someone who can give as well as take. Someone who is gentle and willing to try different things. Slow sometimes, fast sometimes."

Jenn lists three defining characteristics of a good lover: "Trust. Compatibility. And silliness." Suzanne defines a good lover as, "Someone who likes to make love to women. Who likes herself making love to women. And one thing that's really nice is appreciation. Intelligence plays into it, too. But I don't want to discount experience. I've reaped the benefits of very experienced women."

Lydia's ideal lover is "somebody who really loves and enjoys sex. Who has experience and is willing to experiment. Who really wants to make the experience as pleasurable as possible."

Of the abilities and characteristics mentioned by these women, all except experience are available to the newly out lesbian. And if she's willing to express her affection, consideration, enthusiasm, imagination, and ability to listen, she should be able to gain that experience very quickly!

GROUP SEX. For some lesbians, group sex is a dream come true. Imagine kissing one woman and touching another's breasts while a third licks your clit and a fourth nibbles your back. All over the room, women are fucking and licking each other, and their moans fill your ears.

Or imagine just watching.

The best way to start a group scene is by group talking. Make sure everyone knows it's okay to leave or stop at any time. Discuss what safer-sex techniques are to be practiced, if any. Find out what range of vanilla to kinky everyone prefers.

Group sex scenes are enhanced by comfortable surroundings, with plenty of pillows and cushions. All supplies should be at hand, whether lubricants, dildos, whipped cream, or whips. Porn on the VCR or sexy music can help set the mood. There should be plenty of food and drink, too.

If you and your lover want to try group sex together, make sure you are clear about your boundaries and jealousies. (See also *Exhibitionism; Sex Clubs; Threesomes.*)

H

HAPPILY EVER AFTER. For many lesbians, "happily ever after" is the ultimate goal, but how many achieve this dream? That's a difficult question to answer.

Sometimes it seems that *all* lesbian couples have been together less than five years; there is even a widespread belief that "lesbian relationships just don't last." However, that belief is based on those couples who are out and about, who tend to be younger and not yet settled down. Really long-term couples, who tend to be older, may not socialize much in the "lesbian community"; some are totally closeted. In truth, there is no way to know what *most* lesbians are doing since there is no way to know who *most* lesbians are.

Looking to the written history of lesbians, books such as Lillian Faderman's *Odd Girls and Twilight Lovers* and Joan Nestle's *The Persistent Desire* prove that some women *have* achieved "happily ever after," often staying together for decades. And, while it's nice to know what other lesbians are doing and have done, each couple can write their own history for themselves.

If "happily ever after" is your dream, there's no reason you can't work to make it come true. And "happily ever after" does take work.

First, it's important to be realistic about just what this goal means. It doesn't mean "happily every second ever after." Successful long-term couples live together for decades, but those decades are not consistently and smoothly joyous. Relationships include sexual ebbs and flows, compatibility ups and downs, renegotiations when one partner or the other changes her goals or beliefs, outside crushes or even infidelity, health problems, money problems, boredom, and all the other pressures and challenges that life provides. Of course, long-term couples also enjoy comfort, commitment, and companionship, but those benefits aren't at the fore every minute of every day of every year of every decade.

So, how *does* one survive the vicissitudes of life and love to achieve "happily ever after" — or a reasonable facsimile thereof? Simply decide to stick together through thick and thin. No matter what. And live by that decision.

Other ingredients also add to the successful relationship: Having separate friends and interests *and* shared friends and interests. A sense of privacy. A sense of humor. A satisfying sex life. Shared goals and life values. Genuinely liking each other!

But it's that decision to stick together that matters most. Commitment. Commitment says, "I can survive this crisis." Commitment says, "I can live without sex for a while." Commitment says, "This is the woman I choose to be with, even if I find other women attractive." Commitment says, *"This* is my life."

Commitment plus love plus patience will frequently equal long-term joy and peace. (See *Long-Term Relationships; Monogamy.*)

HEALTH.

Doctors. To receive decent health care, lesbians must be informed and assertive patients. Too many doctors know next to nothing about the health care needs of gay women.

If you possibly can, find a lesbian or lesbian-aware doctor. Friends may have recommendations; lesbian and gay centers often offer referrals. Also read the ads in lesbian and gay newspapers. Having a lesbian or lesbian-aware doctor can vastly improve the quality of care you receive.

If you can't find such a doctor, or if you choose not to, pick your health care provider carefully. Most will assume you're heterosexual, and too many will have no idea what lesbians do sexually. When Alice wanted to know if she could have caught an infection from her lover, she had to explain to her doctor that lesbians have oral sex! Alice belonged to a health maintenance organization, and changing doctors was not easy. Luckily, her doctor continued to be concerned about her health after she came out to him; some doctors simply cannot deal with lesbians *at all.*

Because of the ignorance and prejudice of many doctors around lesbian health care, it's important to educate yourself about your health. Read books such as *The New Our Bodies, Ourselves; A New View of a Woman's Body;* and *Alive and Well,* an opinionated but useful guide to lesbian health. Read health-related articles in feminist and lesbian publications. Talk to friends about your concerns.

Legal matters. A major problem for lesbians dealing with the health care establishment is convincing doctors and hospitals to honor their lovers as "next of kin." One helpful step is to have a "medical power of attorney" made up in each other's names (see *A Legal Guide for Lesbian and Gay Couples* or your lawyer). In addition, research what "domestic partner" or "alternate family" laws exist where you live, and take full advantage of whatever rights you do have.

When Kathy had a breast biopsy, she told her surgeon at every appointment that her lover was her next of kin and didn't stop repeating herself until he had clearly and verbally acknowledged their relationship. She then wrote a follow-up letter summarizing their conversation. Kathy and her lover are both out of the closet and secure in their jobs, so this approach was possible for them.

   If this level of openness is not an option for you, and you are facing a major health problem, consider claiming that you and your lover are sisters. This approach can also work if one of you ends up in the hospital after a car accident or for some other emergency. It's okay to be politically incorrect when your lover is in the intensive care unit! Just make sure you agree in advance on your stories and on why you have different last names.

However, this is a temporary solution; as Karen Thompson's sad and infuriating book *Why Can't Sharon Kowalski Come Home?* shows, it is best to establish early on, in as many ways as possible, that you and your lover are a family unit.

Research. Keep up to date with new findings in women's health areas, including sexually transmitted diseases and cancer. Don't accept simplistic statements; read detailed accounts with a critical eye. For instance, if an article announces that lesbians are less likely to get a certain sort of cancer, find out why. The lower cancer rate may be related to not having children or never having slept with men. If you do have children or have slept with men, your health risks will be based on your own activities and history, not on your label.

Also keep up to date on findings about tests and treatments and their side effects. For instance, some doctors believe that mammograms are unnecessary — and even dangerous — in women with no history of breast cancer in their family; others believe that the prevention advantages of mammograms far outweigh their risks. Try to find out *why* doctors hold these different beliefs before coming to your own conclusions.

Health tips. Eating well may be the single most important thing you can do to take care of yourself. Eat lots of fruits and vegetables. Limit your intake of fats, sugar, and caffeine. Make sure you get enough calcium. Avoid consuming too much meat and fried foods. And eat yogurt daily while taking antibiotics to avoid a yeast infection.

Establishing certain simple habits can help you stay healthy with very little effort and cost. Exercise. Avoid direct sunlight or use a good sunscreen. Do your breast self-examination every month! (See also *Breast Self-Examination.)* In addition, be sure to have a Pap test yearly. In this test, the doctor samples cells from your cervix to check for cancer. If you are at high risk for cervical cancer, Pap tests should be repeated every six months.

Cleanliness habits also affect your health. After going to the bathroom, wipe yourself front to back so that you do not bring any fecal germs toward your genitals, where they can cause vaginal and urinary infections. Don't sit directly on public toilet seats; it *is* possible to get some diseases that way. If your knees can't handle squatting, put lots of paper on the seat: if you are going to have a bowel movement, put paper *in* the toilet as well, so that germ-laden toilet water doesn't splash on you.

DES. If your mother took DES (diethylstilbestrol) to avoid miscarrying while she was pregnant with you, you may be at high risk for developing cervical cancer. Make sure your doctor gives you a Schiller test rather than a standard Pap test, educate yourself about DES (Pat Califia's book *Sapphistry* is a good place to start), and keep up to date with new findings about DES daughters. (See also *AIDS; Sexually Transmitted Diseases.*)

HERPES. See *Sexually Transmitted Diseases.*

HETEROSEXUALITY SURVIVORS. Many lesbians have had sex with men when they didn't want to. These women tried heterosexuality to "cure" themselves, to fit in, to retain the love of their families, and because they'd been told that lesbianism "was just a phase they were going through."

Some lesbians enjoy, or don't mind, their experiences with men. Others experiment briefly and move on to women, never looking back. But many lesbians spend years in relationships and marriages they do not want, do not enjoy, and don't know how to get out of. If the world were a place where these women could safely express their homosexuality with the support of their loved ones, those heterosexual relationships would never happen.

Lesbians who survive unwanted heterosexual relationships often feel that a chunk of their lives was stolen from them. They spent years trapped into having sex with men they did not desire, and they expended their precious life energy keeping up a facade to hide their real selves. When such women finally manage to come out, they are relieved and thrilled, but they are also angry. They know they will never get those years back.

Although not an official condition like "incest survivor" or "rape survivor," being a "marriage survivor" or a "forced heterosexuality survivor" is similar. In all of these situations, someone feels that she cannot refuse sex she doesn't want. She may chastise herself for not being able to say no and wonder what is wrong with her. She may suffer damaged self-esteem and self-image.

Now that women come out younger and younger, older heterosexuality survivors may look at them and feel particularly bereft, angry, and guilty. It's too easy in the 1990s to forget the pressures women felt just a few decades ago.

Particularly because being a "marriage survivor" or "forced heterosexuality survivor" is not officially recognized by psychology groups, the issue often goes unaddressed. But it is still a form of coerced sex, demanded by the weight of society saying, *"This is what you must do."* It can be particularly damaging when the victim feels complicit. As a friend of Kathy's said, "I still get angry. I never wanted him. I hated having sex with him. I lost thirteen years. I don't know why I couldn't just come out like other women did, but those thirteen years are gone forever." (See also *Survivors.*)

HISTORY. It is unlikely that a sex book aimed at heterosexuals would bother with an entry on history, since straight people can take their sexuality for granted and have learned about straight heroes their whole lives. However, whatever small freedoms lesbians and gay men enjoy in the United States in the late twentieth century result from years of struggle. As recently as the 1950s, a book like this couldn't even be published. And as recently as last year, many printers refused to print the book *Gay Sex* because of its drawings of men having sex together. Twenty-three states and the District of Columbia retain sodomy laws, some of which only restrict activity between people of the same gender. (For instance, cunnilingus may be legal when a man does it but not when a woman does.) Heterosexuals can separate their sex lives from history; lesbians and gay men cannot.

If animal behavior is any clue, homosexual activity in humans probably arose as soon the species did (see *Bonobos*). Early known homosexuals include Sappho (sixth century B.C.E., Greece), the brilliant lyric poet, and Alexander the Great (356–323 B.C.E.), king of Macedon and tireless conquerer and imperialist. Moving to the more recent past, writers such as Gertrude Stein, Natalie Barney, Virginia Woolf, Djuna Barnes, Willa Cather, and Carson McCullers were all more or less lesbian. Eleanor Roosevelt had a female lover, as did many suffragists and early feminists. Exploration of lesbian history books quickly reveals that where there were women of accomplishment, there were lesbians.

The modern pride movement in the United States is traditionally said to have begun June 28–29, 1969, at New York City's Stonewall Inn, when a group of gay people responded to a police raid by rioting. However, homosexuals had actually begun fighting for better treatment in the United States decades earlier. In 1924, the homosexual Society for Human Rights briefly existed in Illinois; in 1928, Radclyffe Hall published *The Well of Loneliness*, with its groundbreaking plea for tolerance. Lisa Ben (an anagram of "lesbian") began publishing *Vice-Versa*, the first known U.S. lesbian magazine, in 1947. In 1955 Del Martin, Phyllis Lyon, and six other lesbians created the Daughters of Bilitis, a social club that eventually went national and expanded to include political and educational action as well as socializing. The 1960s saw various lesbian and gay picket lines, as unbelievably brave people risked arrest in a uniformly hostile environment. So, while Stonewall provided the movement with a wonderful rallying point, it did not arise out of nowhere; lesbians and gay men had been fighting for our rights for years.

After Stonewall, the pride movement gained momentum like a train getting up a head of steam. First there was one protest here, one newspaper article there. Then the protests grew, the organizations expanded, publishing houses were started, political battles were waged, and more and more people came out of the closet. In 1972, William Johnson became the first openly gay person to be ordained by a major religious denomination. A year later, open lesbian Elaine Noble was elected to the Massachusetts state legislature. In 1974, *Time* magazine put Leonard Matlovich, discharged from the air force for being gay, on the cover. In 1976, a *Doonesbury* character came out. In 1977, *very* openly gay Harvey Milk was elected to the San Francisco Board of Supervisors and two lesbians won child custody cases. In 1978, Proposition 6, banning gay men and lesbians and all positive mentions of homosexuality from schools, was rejected by California voters — and Harvey Milk was assassinated by major homophobe Dan White. In 1979, the first lesbian and gay march on Washington attracted upwards of 100,000 people. By the 1980s, it was clear that the pride movement was here to stay.

When AIDS came into the picture, the movement was hurt and helped. Gay people were blamed for introducing AIDS to the world, and bigots used the disease as another excuse to hate homosexuals. As thousands of gay men died, the pride movement lost countless leaders and friends. However, gay men's and lesbians' anger around AIDS caused many to become more active politically, and their love for their sick friends caused them to become more cohesive emotionally. In addition, the pain and loss in the community made some heterosexuals begin to see that homosexuals are human.

During the 1980s, the pride train gathered a full and hearty head of steam, with more and more lesbian and gay elected officials, lesbian and gay issues covered regularly in large metropolitan newspapers and national magazines, and the occasional positive lesbian or gay character in movies and on TV.

In 1980, open lesbian Karen Clark was elected to the Minnesota House of Representatives. In 1981, California Governor Jerry Brown appointed openly lesbian Mary Morgan to the San Francisco Municipal Court. In 1982, the first international Gay Games were held. In 1983, Congressman Gerry Studds came out. In 1984, Berkeley, California, passed an early domestic partners law. In 1986, Denmark allowed same-gender couples one benefit previously limited to married (hetero) couples: an inheritance tax break. In 1987, Congressman Barney Frank came out; ACT-UP was born; and hundreds of thousands of lesbians and gay men marched on Washington in one of history's largest civil rights gatherings (although the major weekly news magazines didn't see fit to mention it!). In 1988, Sweden granted same-gender couples some tax breaks and social services. In 1989, U.S. Department of Defense studies discovered that gay people are as well suited, if not better, to be in the military as straights (and the Pentagon tried to hide the findings).

In 1990, President George Bush invited gay people to witness his signing of a hate crimes bill, and San Francisco voters approved a domestic partnership law. In 1991, New York City Mayor David Dinkins marched with a gay Irish group that had been denied entry into the St. Patrick's Day Parade; Connecticut became the fourth state with a gay civil rights bill; and openly gay HIV-positive Tom Duane ran against openly lesbian Liz Abzug in a New York City Council race (Duane won). In 1992, lesbians and gay men tightened the pressure on the military to admit and retain open lesbians and gay men; presidential candidates wooed the gay vote; lesbian heartthrob k.d. lang came out; the State Supreme Court overturned the Kentucky sodomy law; and Vermont passed a bill prohibiting antigay discrimination in hiring, housing, and finances.

In the 1990s and beyond, lesbians and gay men everywhere will still be fighting for a larger voice in government, more positive depictions of gay people in movies and on TV, freedom to stay in the military, the right to get married, and all the other rights that straight people take for granted. Our history is still being written, and only we can make sure there is a happy ending.

HIV. (Human Immunodeficiency Virus; the suspected cause or one of the causes of AIDS.) See *AIDS; Safer Sex; Sexually Transmitted Diseases.*

HOMOPHOBIA. The word *homophobia* is a relatively recent addition to the English language, although the problem has been around for centuries. A *phobia* is an abnormal or illogical fear; *homophobia* is an abnormal or illogical fear of homosexuals. Some lesbians and gay men prefer *homohatred* as a more honest word. But *homophobia* has caught on, so it is the term we are stuck with, at least for now.

The idea of homophobia is familiar to any gay woman who lives in the real world. Homophobia is why lesbians cannot marry, why lesbians can be fired from jobs in most places just for being gay, and why lesbians are at risk of violence if we hold hands on the street. Homophobia is why lesbians are "disappeared" from history books and TV shows. Homophobia is why so many lesbians spend years in glum misery, wondering if we will ever get to love a woman.

Unfortunately, homophobia damages all lesbians, one way or another. Since gay girls generally cannot date other gay girls when we are teens, the growth lessons of adolescence are replaced with fear and self-hatred. And, since lesbians have most often been represented in literature, art, movies, and TV as ugly and evil perverts, young gay women lack positive images of themselves. Most importantly, as lesbians grow up surrounded by homophobia, we take that hatred in and all too often believe it; this is known as *internalized homophobia.*

Internalized homophobia shows up in a million ways. When a lesbian accepts her family's belief that her brother's heterosexual relationship is more important than her homosexual one, that's internalized homophobia. When a lesbian sees heterosexuals as individuals and homosexuals as stereotypes ("Why do they have to dress like that?!"), that's internalized homophobia. And when a lesbian, deep down inside, feels dirty and disgusting because she has sex with women, that's internalized homophobia.

Unsurprisingly, internalized and external homophobia both wreak havoc on sex lives. The mother who fears losing her children if her ex-husband finds out she's involved with a woman may be unable to relax and enjoy herself making love. The lesbian who believes herself dirty, disgusting, and unattractive will have trouble accepting that someone loves and desires her. And the lesbian brought up in a homophobic religion may fear divine retribution for having sex.

Curing internalized homophobia takes time and positive input. Read lesbian novels. Find lesbian friends. Join lesbian and gay groups. Use positive affirmations. And give yourself a break. Even the most pro-lesbian, out-there, committed dyke occasionally finds herself having a homophobic reflex. Since millions of people hate homosexuals, it can be hard to hear that internal voice saying, "I'm okay." But being a lesbian is wonderful. And if millions of people disagree, then those millions of people are wrong. (See also *Coming Out.*)

HOTLINES. Hotlines offer a variety of services, from providing information to counseling potential suicides. You can call a lesbian and gay hotline to find when an organization meets or where the nearest lesbian bar is. Call for support, help, or the name of a good lesbian novel or pro-gay therapist. Call just to hear a friendly *gay* voice.

To track down a lesbian and gay hotline, check the listings and classified ad sections of lesbian and gay newspapers. Or look in the phone book under "lesbian," "gay," "women's," "lavender," "lambda," and "hotline." If necessary, try again with your area's name in front of those words: for instance, "Oshkosh lesbian," "Sarasota gay," or "Louisville women's."

If these approaches fail, try the nearest large city. If you are feeling isolated, even a long-distance phone call to a gay or lesbian stranger can remind you that you are not alone.

I–K

INCEST SURVIVORS. See *Survivors.*

INTERNALIZED HOMOPHOBIA. See *Homophobia.*

INTIMACY. (A high level of emotional openness and affection.)

For some people, the goal of sex is intimacy; for others, intimacy just gets in the way. If two people disagree on intimacy goals, neither is wrong and neither is right, but they may never have satisfying sex together.

To understand intimacy's place in lesbian sex, we have to break away from myths and brainwashing. Most women are taught that only sluts enjoy nonintimate sex, but that's an old husbands' tale. Wanting sex for sex's sake does not make a woman dirty or evil, and it's probably time to retire — or redefine — words like *slut* altogether.

There is nothing wrong or immoral with occasionally — or always — having sex for fun, for relaxation, or just for the hell of it. In addition, women dealing with incest, molestation, and rape issues — or with intimacy issues — may sometimes prefer limited sexual openness to keep from becoming overwhelmed. Optimal intimacy levels, like everything else in sex, are personal choices, with no one's desires better or worse than anyone else's. Most of us will find that our desires vary at different times and in different situations.

Striving for intimacy. If you seek more intimacy in your sex life, have patience. No two people achieve instant intimacy; like trust, intimacy needs nurturance and a suitable, safe environment. Over time, your ability to be intimate can grow daily (perhaps with occasional setbacks).

If you love and trust your partner, intimacy may bloom naturally; if, however, you have survived an abusive childhood or just generally have trouble trusting people, achieving intimacy may require more work or even therapy.

For detailed information on how to achieve intimacy, see the self-help section of any bookstore. (See also *Casual Sex; Emotions.*)

JEALOUSY. Jealousy is a difficult, mean, paradoxical emotion that can ruin sex and destroy relationships. It's particularly inconvenient in the lesbian community, where so many women remain friends with their ex-lovers.

It would seem that there are two sorts of jealousy: (1) jealousy without cause and (2) jealousy with cause. For instance, if a woman is jealous of her partner's ex-lover, that emotion will make more "sense" if the partner actually does have sex with the ex. But jealousy is not a thing of logic, nor can it be addressed with simple notions of right and wrong.

A worst-case scenario is when one lover becomes jealous of the other's friends, job, fantasies, and interests, wanting the woman all to herself in every way. The possessive lover lives in constant pain, and the possessed lover feels like she is in jail. This level of jealousy will kill a relationship.

But say a woman does have reason to be jealous. Say her partner had sex outside a relationship that they had agreed would be monogamous. Although the wronged woman has every reason to be upset, if she wants to retain the relationship she must eventually let go of her jealousy. Jealousy, whether legitimate or not, strangles trust, hope, love, and second chances. And sometimes it's less important to be right than to be happy.

But what if, with reason or without, a person just can't help being jealous? If she wants to be in a couple, she must change. Therapy may be in order. Jealousy is poison. (See also *Privacy; Trust.*)

JEWELRY. Years ago, lesbians wore pinky rings to let other lesbians know who they were; some still do. As time passed and the lesbian community came further and further out of the closet, gay women designed lesbian jewelry, with lambdas, women's symbols, labryses, pink and black triangles, naked women, and rainbows prominently displayed.

Nowadays, members of different lesbian subcommunities may wear different jewelry. Stereotypically speaking (and there are many exceptions), "professional women" dress for success, with appropriate jewelry; feminists who came out in the 1970s and early 1980s wear triangles, women's symbols, and Native American designs; and punk queers wear five or six earrings in each ear, plus rings in their pierced noses, nipples, eyebrows, and even tongues. Wear whatever jewelry you like, and you'll be in style somewhere.

Safety warning: Take off large rings during sex if you're going to penetrate your partner. For fisting, it may be wise to take off your bracelets too. (See also *Body Art; Symbols.*)

KEGEL EXERCISES. Once upon a time, a Dr. Arnold Kegel invented pubococcygeal muscle exercises for women who suffered from urinary incontinence. The exercises worked, and they had a lovely side effect; after weeks of doing them, the women reported enhanced pleasure during sex.

The pubococcygeal (PC) muscle is in the lower pelvis, surrounding the opening of the vagina and the urethra. It is the muscle that contracts to stop peeing; it also contracts during orgasms.

The exercises are simple. First, to locate the muscle, pee with your legs apart. Stop the flow; the muscle you use is your PC muscle. Later, lie down, put a finger in your vagina, and try to squeeze it, without squeezing your thighs, butt, or stomach. That's the PC muscle again.

For one Kegel exercise, squeeze your PC for three seconds, then relax it for three seconds, then squeeze it for three seconds, and so on. Three times a day, do ten of these contractions. If you can't hold three-second squeezes at first, do the best you can. As your PC muscle strengthens, the contractions will become easier.

In another Kegel exercise, squeeze and relax, squeeze and relax, as before, only quickly. This, too, should be done in ten-repetition sets, three times a day.

While you don't have to go to the gym or use weights to do Kegels, they are real exercises; don't overdo repetitions, or you may find yourself with a sore PC muscle. However, once you've reached a good, strong, toned state, you can do fifteen or twenty repetitions per set or do more sets each day. Do them at work, while you watch TV, standing on line to pay for groceries, or whenever you think of them. Doing them during sex may intensify your pleasure.

Some women reach a point of PC fitness where they can achieve orgasms simply by doing their Kegels. Now, *that* is an interesting way to pass the time at the supermarket.

KINSEY REPORT. (A compilation and examination of survey data from 8,000 women published in 1953 under the title *Sexual Behavior in the Human Female.*)

Statistics quoted from "the Kinsey report" usually come from the *male* Kinsey report, or *Sexual Behavior in the Human Male.* The oft-cited "fact" that 10 percent of humans are homosexual actually refers only to male humans — and ignores another 27 percent of men who had experienced orgasms with other men. So that famous 10 percent tells us little about men and nothing about women.

What Kinsey did have to say about "human females" is fascinating. By age forty-five, 13 percent of the women in Kinsey's survey had had sexual contact with another woman to orgasm; an additional 7 percent had had some sexual contact with a woman; another 8 percent "recognized erotic responses to other females." In other words, a total of 28 percent of the women acknowledged some homosexuality.

Three to eight percent of unmarried women (based on their experiences at ages twenty to thirty-five) rated 4 (predominantly homosexual with "a fair amount of overt heterosexual contact"), 5 (with "some overt heterosexual contact"), or 6 (with "no overt heterosexual contact") on the Kinsey scale. One percent of married women and 4 percent to 7 percent of previously married women fit the same categories.

Unfortunately, there is no sure way to extrapolate from these data to the present day; it would be difficult even to reconcile 1953's definition of "homosexual" with today's "lesbian" or "gay woman."

Interestingly, of the 142 women (approximately 1.8 percent) in the report with "the most extensive" homosexual backgrounds, 71 percent reported that they had *no* regrets about their experiences — an astonishingly high percentage considering that they faced almost total social opprobrium, with no positive books, role models, or organizations to turn to!

Kinsey pooh-poohed the fear that homosexuality threatened the survival of the human race, pointing to the myriad other mammalian species in which homosexual behavior and rampant reproduction existed side by side. His list of animals in which female homosexuality has been documented includes "rats, mice, hamsters, guinea pigs, rabbits, porcupines, marten, cattle, antelope, goats, horses, pigs, lions, sheep, monkeys, and chimpanzees." (How interesting that some people still claim that homosexuality does not occur "in nature" when this information has been available for forty years!)

Kinsey viewed female homosexuality as a sometimes useful replacement for heterosexuality, as in career women who didn't have time for marriage, and he noted that "considerable affection or strong emotional attachments were involved in many of these relationships."

Comparing heterosexual with homosexual sex, Kinsey reported that, in the fifth year of married sex, 40 percent of women reached orgasm all the time or nearly all the time; however, in "more extensive homosexual experience," 68 percent of women did. He amusingly concluded that, "Heterosexual relationships could become more satisfactory if they more often utilized the sort of knowledge which most homosexual females have of female sexual anatomy and female psychology." (See also *Bonobos.)*

KISSING. Kisses come in so many sizes and shapes that they should almost have individual names. Compare the soft, dry nibble to the open-mouthed tongues-entwined practically-falling-into-each-other's-faces gobble. They inspire different sensations and they carry different messages. But these types of kisses, and the dozens in between, are all glorious forms of mouth-to-mouth communication.

Like many other facets of sex, kissing takes a certain amount of finesse and choreography. Although it sometimes feels right to jump on each other, tongues flailing away, many women prefer a more gradual build. Start with the smallest of kisses. The intensity of sensation resulting from one set of lips lightly brushing another can

be staggering. Don't rush to the next stage (unless, of course, you really want to). Slip in the tiniest bit of tongue, the slightest touch of teeth. At some point, your mouths will probably melt together and make their own decisions as to what comes next. Enjoy!

Different women kiss in different ways. Some women are bored by little kisses, while others crave them. Some women don't much like tongue kissing. Also, different women hold their mouths and shape their lips in different ways. Some are aggressive with their tongues, while others are more subtle.

Early kissing with a new partner affords a wonderful time for exploration and discovery. Compromise may be called for. Occasionally, two women cannot find a mutual kissing style that works for both of them. That's too bad, but it doesn't have to be the end of the world. They can search for other things they enjoy doing together, whether touching each other, hugging, or playing pool or talking.

Some women experience limits to their kissing because of allergies or physical problems. Solutions can be as simple as keeping kisses short so that you can breathe in between or making sure there are extra pillows around for support. With creativity, determination, and imagination, kissing should be possible.

Interestingly enough, JoAnn Loulan found that 9 percent of her survey respondents did *not* list kissing as a "usual, frequent, or constant" sexual practice (see her book *Lesbian Passion)*. But lesbians who do enjoy kissing often adore the practice.

Suzanne says, "I like kissing. I like soft-lipped kissing, slow kissing, fast kissing. I like French kissing. I like soft lips and breasts mushing up together slowly, and surprising yourself with how warm and nice that feels. Sometimes, one of the things that's really the most exciting is taking a few minutes and just kissing each other. Just kissing each other in the middle of the day and then just going, mmmmmmmm. A real, nice, mushy, soft kiss."

L

LAUGHTER. Our movie brainwashing teaches that sex has to unfold smoothly and gracefully. Blouses slip off, zippers unzip without a hitch, and no one ever has to go to the bathroom.

But real-life sex is like the rest of real life: messy. Passion does occasionally carry people on endless waves of graceful sensuality, but more often, you trip on your pants, she squeezes the lube tube too hard and splashes you with glop, or, horror of horrors, you have to fart while she's going down on you. What's the best way to deal with these mishaps? Laugh.

Laughing together can be as intimate as sex itself, and the message laughter sends is, It's okay, we can deal with anything. Nor is laughter inappropriate to sex; when you think about it, expressing your love by licking each other's private parts is a funny way to spend time (although it can feel downright sacred while it's happening!).

And laughter is a wonderful physical experience in and of itself. It provides a major release of tension, not unlike orgasm, and it relaxes people physically and psychically. For the woman who just got home from work or has been depressed or has been studying nonstop, a good laugh may knock down some emotional walls and enable a freer sexual experience.

Many women consider sex with laughter to be a peak experience. As Kathy recalls, "With Leslie, it seemed that every time we made love, the news would come on the radio. One time, just as we got going, kissing passionately and tearing off each other's clothes, there was one of those reports, you know, 'major earthquake kills dozens, violence against the elderly increases, Liz Taylor to marry again.' What could we do but laugh? We got hysterical. And it turned out to be some of the best sex we ever had."

Jenn's list of the characteristics that make a good lover highlights the importance of laughter: "Trust. Compatibility. And silliness."

LEATHER. Leather turns on many lesbians, whether or not they are into S/M. Some enjoy owning a simple black leather jacket, which they occasionally wear during sex, while others have entire leather sex wardrobes including pants, chaps, miniskirts, wristbands, and boots. Still other women, particularly those who see it as a reflection of patriarchy and violence, are flat-out offended by the use of leather in sex.

Leather can serve as a costume or a prop. Suzanne finds the very presence of leather to be a turn-on: "One of my fantasies that my ex-lover and I played out was making love while she wore her leather jacket and nothing else. It was really quite nice — and very sexy." For Lydia, leather is part of S/M: "I have leather restraints. Nice, soft, solid leather restraints, and I love to be tied up with them."

Vegetarian Jessica feels ambivalent about leather: "I have mixed feelings, but I do find it attractive. Synthetic leather is fine too. I have a pair of black boots, they're totally man-made. I like having that look without having a dead animal on my feet." (See also *Sadomasochism.*)

LEGAL MATTERS.

Sodomy and gay rights laws. In twenty-three states and the District of Columbia, sodomy is illegal. Definitions of *sodomy* vary; the dictionary includes anal sex, oral sex, sex with someone of the same gender, and sex with an animal. The treatment of lesbians and gay men can range from harassment to arrest; in even the most seemingly liberal of locations, police still occasionally find excuses to check IDs at gay bars. In many states, sodomy laws restrict behavior in one's own home: the Supreme Court has ruled that the constitution affords homosexuals *no* legal right to privacy.

It's important to know what the climate is for gay people where you live; an excellent place to start your research is *The Rights of Lesbians and Gay Men: The Basic ACLU Guide to a Gay Person's Rights.* Read local newspapers to monitor any changes; the specifics of legal and illegal discrimination vary from country to country, state to state, city to city, and year to year.

Just because a state doesn't have a sodomy law doesn't mean that you're safe to be openly lesbian. Unless your locale also has some sort of gay rights law, you will still risk losing your job or apartment if you come out publicly. Worst of all, some locales are now passing laws specifically making gay rights illegal. Obviously, fighting for lesbian and gay equality is terribly important.

Legitimizing relationships. Denmark is the only country in the entire world that allows same-gender marriage. You may be with the same woman for twenty years, but you will still have fewer rights than a heterosexual couple married for one day. Here and there, in little pockets of sane humanity, corporations and municipalities are granting same-sex couples shared medical benefits or bereavement leave, but these instances are rare. In the vast majority of cases, you and your lover will have no more legal rights than two strangers.

To protect yourselves as much as possible, make out wills, powers of attorney, partnership agreements, co-parenting agreements, and whatever other paperwork seems appropriate. Go to a lawyer who has experience working with same-gender couples, or see *A Legal Guide for Lesbian and Gay Couples*, by Hayden Curry and Denis Clifford.

Don't underestimate the importance of this paperwork. As related in *Why Can't Sharon Kowalski Come Home?* (by Karen Thompson and Julie Andrzejewski), when Thompson's lover Kowalski was seriously injured in a car accident, Kowalski's parents forbade Thompson to even *visit* Kowalski. Thompson went to court, again and again and again, and discovered just how many legal rights lesbians *don't* have. A few trips to a lawyer now may someday save you the years of hell that Thompson and Kowalski have gone through.

LONELINESS. Sometimes, loneliness feels like a fatal disease, and there is a particular loneliness to being a lesbian without lesbian friends.

But what if you've been out for a while, maybe had a lover or two, but now you're alone and you're dreadfully, terribly, painfully lonely? There are a few ways to look at this problem. First of all, some truth: despite the occasional glorification of independence and adventure, the lesbian community tends to travel two-by-two to meetings, dances, restaurants, and parties. A single woman will frequently find herself the only uncoupled woman in a room. And that can feel very lonely indeed.

But the answer is not to run out and find a lover. Yes, having a lover may make you feel better, at least at first, but choosing someone out of loneliness can lead to a painful, mismatched relationship. The cliche is true: being lonely with someone is even worse than being lonely alone.

Dealing with loneliness in a healthy manner involves a two-pronged attack. One prong is to find more friends. If one turns out to be a future lover, great, but having friends is a strong foundation for a full social and emotional life. The other prong is to learn to enjoy your own company. Treat yourself as well and as lovingly as you would a girlfriend, and you may find that much of your loneliness dissipates. If you want to go to the movies, go. If you want to eat at a nice restaurant, do it.

There is another sort of loneliness — or aloneness — the loneliness of choice. Many women find that they need a year or two off after a breakup to heal, work on themselves, and generally regain their balance. These breaks from relationships can be productive, wonderful times.

Ironically, the better you are at being alone, the better your chances of being happily paired. First of all, people are attracted to self-confidence. Second, if you're not in a rush to find just anyone to be with, you can wait for someone you know, like, and respect. (See also *Casual Sex; Dating; Masturbation; Meeting People*.)

LONG-TERM RELATIONSHIPS. A major challenge in long-term relationships is keeping sex lively and exciting. So many lesbian couples suffer from sex falloff that there is a slang name for it: "lesbian bed death." But there are many ways to avoid this problem.

One approach is to make sex dates together. Although this may seem anti-spontaneous, it doesn't have to be. Jenn says, "With appointments, our sex has actually been *more* spontaneous because we know we have enough time to do what we want."

But what if the appointment time comes and you're just not in the mood? Or if you *are* having sex regularly, but it's just not that great? Add variety to what you do. Lie naked together and talk. Have an evening where you only stroke each other, no orgasms allowed. Or make the usual erogenous zones off-limits; focus on toes, the backs of knees, elbows, and ankles. Sometimes a direct approach works; one of you can simply start going down on the other, after minimal foreplay, while she lies there and just enjoys herself, or fantasizes, or maybe reads an erotic story out loud. Try quickies in unusual locations. Rent porn movies. Have sex without making noise — or don't use your hands — or don't get undressed.

Discuss your fantasies and, if you want to, act them out. Try bondage or blindfolds. Go to a bar separately and pick each other up. Imagine your lover is visiting from out of town: what special place would you take her? Or make believe it's your first date and you want to make a great impression.

Whether you keep sex simple or act out every fantasy you have, it's important to give sex a special, even sacred, place in your lives. Don't interrupt foreplay with discussions of dirty dishes, problems with the kids, troubles at work, or the state of the world. Make your bed off-limits for mundane kvetching (see also *Beds*). Don't use your lover as a therapist.

And don't turn on the TV as soon as you get home. (See also *Communication; Romance.*)

LOOKING. While some women prefer to make love in the dark, others enjoy having enough light to really look at one another.

Staring into your lover's eyes can be magnificent foreplay, as can observing the way her muscles flex as she undresses. The lines of a woman's neck, shoulder blades, breasts, and thighs are as beautiful as anything in nature or on view in a museum. And watching your partner masturbate to orgasm can be as sexy as coming yourself.

Jessica says, "I love to watch — to keep an eye on what she's doing and what I'm doing. One woman I slept with had the most incredibly pink cunt — bright pink. I would just sit there and go, 'Oh it's so beautiful! I'm having so much fun!'"

LOVE VERSUS BEING IN LOVE. "Being in love" is that wonderful, early, insane feeling, when you and your partner cannot keep your hands off each other and all seems perfect. It's nine parts chemicals and one part dreams, and it's the most fun you can have and still be human. But it doesn't last. It can't. If it did, businesses would grind to a halt, governments would collapse, and traffic would stop as everyone stayed at home, in bed, with the person she was in love with.

In time, "being in love" either grows into garden-variety love (which is still a gift, a blessing, and a miracle) or it fizzles out.

Whereas being in love constantly sizzles, regular love does not feel hot and exciting every second; after the thrill of being in love, the first nonsexual lull may feel like death. But lapses in intensity are part of real life; love, unlike being in love, requires the occasional time-out.

The longer a love lasts, the more challenges it faces. From crushes on other women to dealing with relatives to differing work hours to bad moods to PMS to ebbs and flows in sexuality, the list of potential problems is endless. Yet a good strong love can sustain two women through the buffeting winds of real life.

What are the ingredients that nourish love? Some people cite good sexual rapport. Others point to a sense of humor and the ability to let things go. Still others argue that a couple must simply like and enjoy each other.

The complete formula for long-term love probably looks something like this:

love = friendship + sex + commitment + compatibility
+ support from friends + a sense of humor + *luck*

LUBRICATION. Many women produce sufficient vaginal lubrication for all their sexual needs. But some women are naturally less wet than others, and stress, phases in the menstrual cycle, menopause, and certain medications can lessen the amount of natural lubrication a woman produces. In addition, extra lubrication eases certain sexual practices, including fisting and anal penetration.

A range of commercial lubricants is available. Probe, which can be purchased at sex shops and through the mail (see *Mail Order)*, is a big favorite. It's marvelously slippery, it doesn't taste bad, and it stays fairly warm sitting in its container. (If a lubricant is cold, pour it onto your hands and let it get warm before putting it anywhere else — unless, of course, you prefer the cold.) K-Y Jelly is also popular and can be found at most pharmacies and supermarkets.

There are brands of commercial lubes that offer special features. Some come in flavors, while others heat up on your skin. Always test-drive a specialty lube by dabbing a bit on your knee or arm before putting it in your vagina or anus. If you are allergic to it or don't like the way it feels, it's best to find that out in an accessible, external location that can be quickly washed.

Similarly, flavored lubes should be taste-tested. Some of them are pretty gross, and Jenn says that one brand made her tongue go numb.

Avoid petroleum jelly and other non-water-soluble substances for lubrication. They are difficult to clean out of your vagina, and they weaken condoms, dental dams, and rubber gloves.

M–N

MAIL ORDER. If your locale lacks gay stores, you can easily buy lesbian and gay books, magazines, movies, videos, and gay pride paraphernalia from the privacy of your home. For example, you can mail-order lesbian and gay books from Lambda Rising or A Different Light, and specific publishers regularly distribute catalogues of their wares.

The company Sapphile sends out regular lesbian- and gay-related group mailings; a recent packet included information on cruises, magazines, t-shirts, music, and businesses. If you are in the closet, however, be warned that they do not use the proverbial "plain brown wrapper"; anyone with knowledge about gay symbols and history will know from the envelope that Sapphile is a gay outfit.

Through personal ads, one can even find a lover through the mail. (See *Personal Ads.)*

And if you don't want to go to the local "adult bookstore" to buy your sex supplies — toys, lubricants, and sex writing and videos — Good Vibrations in San Francisco and Eve's Garden in New York are both worth investigating. Not only do these places provide wonderful sexual materials, but their employees also answer questions and provide further information. Their blasé attitude is most comforting; ordering dildos by phone need not be any more anxiety-producing than ordering tickets to a ball game.

If you should find yourself in San Francisco or New York, do visit these stores — and also look for sex toy exhibits at women's music festivals. It really is best to choose between a corncob-shaped dildo and a dolphin-shaped dildo in person. (See the *Resource List.)*

MAKING LOVE. Although commonly used as synonyms, *making love* and *having sex* are not identical. Many women enjoy sex without love, and lovemaking without sex can also be great fun.

There are dozens of ways to express love physically: Cuddling and stroking. Backrubs and full-body massages. Making out. Back scratches. And that old favorite, footrubs.

Making love nonsexually can save relationships that are going through sexual ebbs. Perhaps one partner is dealing with incest issues. Perhaps the other is working too hard. Perhaps both just aren't in the mood. Sex sometimes ends up on the back burner, but why should sensuality join it there? Nonsexual lovemaking reassures both partners that their connection still exists, plus it feels good.

MAKING NOISE. Moans and groans add another dimension to sex. If the senses of taste, touch, smell, and sight are all being entertained, why shouldn't hearing have some fun too?

The smallest sex noises can provoke large responses all over your body. Whispered "ooohs" stand hairs on end, set skin tingling, and start labia swelling. Coming noises — moans, groans, growls, and yells — can make the other lover feel like she's coming too.

Sex noises are great toys that you can play with at odd times. At the supermarket, lean into her ear and murmur, "Oh, oh, ooh, oooooh, *oooooh,*" and you may unpack more than groceries when you get home. Or try sex without making any noise at all, and see how vocal energy can reshape itself into orgasmic energy. If you have children or for some other reason lack the privacy to make all the noise you want, try occasionally to sneak home early from work or go to a hotel and moan your heads off. *All* your sexual parts should get to express themselves now and again.

For some reason, a legend once sprang into existence that noisy women are hotter lovers than quiet women. In response, a counter-legend sprang up to insist that making noise is just showing off, while silence evidences *true* sexual intensity. Is this debate silly or what?

If you're noisy during sex, great. If you're not, great. Yes, noisy women may have to temper themselves when they lack privacy. And, yes, quiet women may find that their lovers grow insecure because they're not oohing and aahing and oh-baby-ing. But these problems can be solved with a reasonable amount of communication and compromise.

But what if the problems are more serious? What if one woman is embarrassed by her partner's noisiness? Or the other woman feels bereft of a deeper level of intimacy because her lover is quiet? Again, try communication and compromise, and a balanced accord may be reached. If not, perhaps the disagreement around noisemaking is masking larger problems. Not every two women are compatible sexually. If compromise seems impossible and your noisemaking needs are that important to you, find someone who meets them; you deserve to express yourself as you desire.

MANNERS. Emily Vanderbilt never devoted a chapter to who sleeps in the wet spot when two women become lovers. Is it okay to ask for the left side of the bed? Why is it difficult to use your partner's toothbrush when you just had her vulva in your mouth? Should the window stay open or closed? Is it acceptable to request that the dog sleep in another room?

Since there are no definite answers to these questions, and since every couple interacts differently, only guidelines are possible here. Guideline #1: if you're not sure, ask. Guideline #2: have a sense of

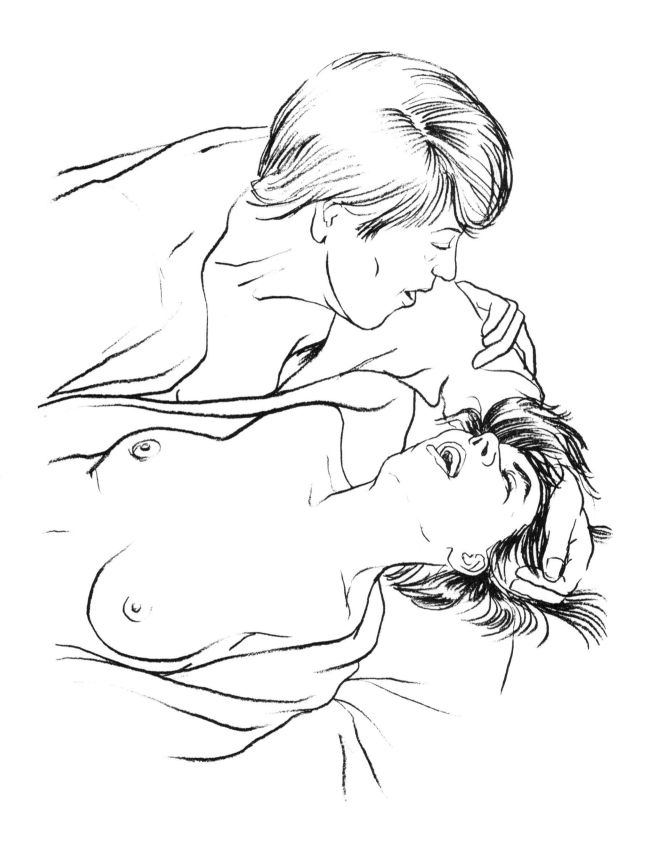

humor. Guideline #3: don't be unnecessarily stoic; if you end up on the wet spot, ask for a towel. Guideline #4: there are no wrongs and no rights when it comes to cleanliness, sleeping habits, and household arrangements, and compromise is (nearly) always possible. Guideline #5: when it comes to her dog or cat, be careful. A woman who adores you, who has just shared twenty orgasms with you, who seems sane in every respect, can turn mean if you don't like her pet.

MARRIAGE. Homosexual marriages are not legal (except in Denmark), but more and more same-gender couples are having commitment ceremonies. These ceremonies range from informal declarations of love followed by a picnic in the backyard to clergy-run rites with catered dinners and reception lines afterward. The women's families may be involved. When Jenn and her lover had a holy union ceremony, Jenn says, "my mom catered it, and all three of my sisters flew out from back East."

Lesbians fall into three schools of thought about these ceremonies. Some women love the idea and would leap at the chance of getting married legally. Others despise the very thought of marriage, seeing it as more about property ownership and patriarchy than love and commitment. Still other women find the ceremonies a silly, pointless idea — until they go to one; then they congratulate the couple, tears in their eyes, saying, "I had no idea I'd be so moved."

Having an official commitment ceremony offers many benefits to a couple. There is something concrete and serious about saying "I love you" in front of caring witnesses, and an official ceremony may help the couple to banish the last bits of internalized homophobia that insist a same-sex relationship is less important than an opposite-sex one. Also, the ceremony gives lesbian and gay friends, who seem to most often assemble for protests and funerals, the opportunity to gather for a joyous occasion. What could be more beautiful than having friends share your happiness?

If you're interested in a religious ceremony, some mainstream churches and synagogues will cooperate. If no larger religious institution near you does same-gender ceremonies, ask around for sympathetic clergy; often individuals are more advanced than institutions. Also investigate MCC (Metropolitan Community Church) and other lesbian and gay religious organizations, such as Dignity and Integrity.

When planning your commitment ceremony, talk to couples who have already had one. These couples may know gay-owned or gay-friendly caterers, printers, restaurants, or other businesses that will not hassle you for being lesbians. They may also know which lesbian and gay paper (or, rarely, mainstream daily) will print commitment announcements.

Since same-sex ceremonies are such a recent invention, you are not beholden to tradition. Invent yours from scratch to suit yourselves. Pick your favorite music and poetry. Dress as you please. Have a friend or religious leader do the ceremony or do it yourselves. Make the event your dream come true. (See also *Legal Matters*.)

MARRIAGE SURVIVORS. See *Heterosexuality Survivors; Survivors*.

MASSAGE. Massage is a sure way to her heart, but if you make her too relaxed and sleepy, it may not be a sure way to other places. In general, when using massage as foreplay, mix rubbing and kneading with kissing and stroking. While massaging her back, for instance, kiss down the length of her spine. While massaging her buttocks or thighs, slip a gentle hand between her legs. All over her body, vary strong kneading motions with tender nibbles. While a relaxation massage may focus on her back, a sexual massage will tend more toward her front. Massage her breasts gently, or harder if she prefers.

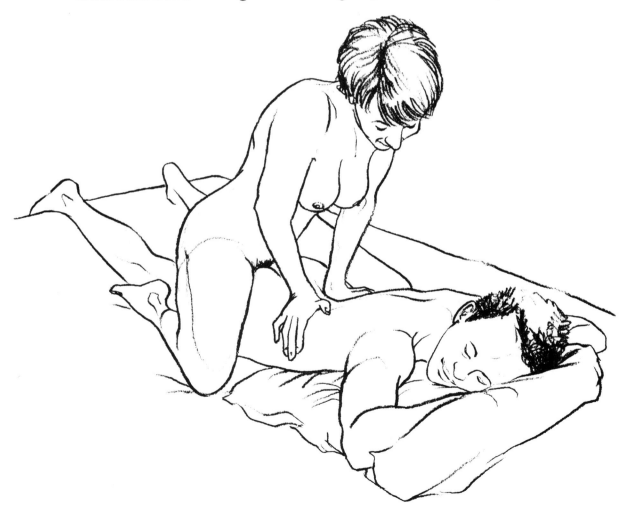

Massage her belly and ovaries and inner thighs. Combine approaches, as in massaging her belly while licking her breasts. Making someone relax *and* get turned on takes a bit of skill, but it's well worth practicing.

The Art of Erotic Massage, by Andrew Yorke, discusses all sorts of techniques for pleasuring your partner; however, the book is hyper-heterosexual.

MASTECTOMY. With breast cancer rates at one woman in nine, you may well end up making love with someone who has had a mastectomy or having one yourself. Mastectomies affect women's health, attitudes, social life, body image, and sexuality.

If it's you. If you experience a mastectomy, you may feel tired from treatment, terrified of the cancer, and low on positive body image. You may decide to have your breast reconstructed — or you may not. You may experience a loss of sexual desire — or you may not. If you don't have a lover, you may fear never finding one again. If you're in a relationship, you may need more than ever to know your lover finds you attractive — but you probably won't want to feel pressured to have sex. Or you may want to go on with your love life as though nothing has happened.

Although articles have been written about "the woman's response to mastectomy," each woman is an individual with individual reactions. You have the right to feel whatever you feel, without fitting into some pre-existing profile.

Your friends may not be able to give you all the emotional sustenance you need, and you may want to see a therapist or join a support group of women who have had mastectomies. Ask your doctor or women's center where to find one. You may be able to locate a lesbian group.

If you've had a mastectomy and are about to sleep with a new woman — or if you're going to have sex with your longtime lover for the first time after the operation — you're likely to be nervous. Talk to your partner, and be honest about your needs. Listen to hers as well. If you want to keep a shirt on, or go slowly, or go quickly, or whatever, tell her. If you don't know what you want, tell her that too.

Although you may fear that women will no longer find you attractive, many will. Rebecca had a mastectomy years ago, and the additional treatment she underwent weakened her heart. She devotes much of her time and money to health care and says that her sex life has changed because she doesn't have the energy she once had. However, her sexual experiences after her mastectomy have been consistently positive: "When I first learned I was going to have a mastectomy, the straight women I knew were horrified by the loss of the breast. They said things like, 'If it was me, I'd kill myself.' And I thought, I'm glad I'm a lesbian. Looksism *is* an issue of lesbians, but nowhere to the same degree. It's amazing to me the beautiful, wonderful women who have wanted to sleep with me. I know that my mastectomy had to be an issue for them, but, except for one woman — and that wasn't a sexual issue — they never let me know. They just never did."

If your partner has a mastectomy. If your lover has a mastectomy, you will, of course, be tremendously affected; although the operation happens to only one of you, the experience happens to both. Sexually, you may vacillate between wanting to make love and being scared of rushing her. In addition, you may fear touching her changed body and have many questions: Will she want to make love more gently than she used to? Will she want her remaining breast touched or ignored?

This is an important time for you to talk to each other honestly and acknowledge what you are going through. Discuss what you want and expect from sex — and also discuss your fears. You will probably both need reassurance that you still want and desire each other, even though your sex life may change.

Consider also talking to friends or a therapist, together or separately.

Dating. If you start having sex with a woman who has had a mastectomy, don't treat her like an invalid. If you are not sure how she wants to make love, ask her — but in terms of her whole self, not in terms of her being "a-woman-missing-a-breast." She may want to go slowly and make love semidressed — or she may want to jump right in and have sex totally nude. She may want her breast area ignored or paid attention to. She may prefer quiet, intense sex or wild, abandoned sex. Women who have had mastectomies vary as much as any other women. (See also *Breast Self-Examination.)*

MASTURBATION. (Stimulating one's clitoris, vulva, vagina, anus, or breasts, usually to orgasm.)

Like all types of sex, masturbation can range from a tension-releasing quickie to the culmination of a romantic evening that includes dinner by candlelight or a movie. Despite the myths of our childhoods, masturbation does not harm us; if it did, 98 percent of the people on earth would be blind and blemished with hairy palms. In reality, masturbation offers a positive way to learn about our bodies, to express love for ourselves, and to relieve tension (sexual and otherwise).

Some women masturbate frequently, others rarely or never. Masturbation habits evolve over a lifetime, depending on whether you are healthy, feeling sexual in general, distracted by work or school, dealing with past abuse, and in or out of a relationship. Single lesbians don't all masturbate frequently, and partnered lesbians don't all quit masturbating. Regular sex stimulates some women into a general state of arousal, increasing their interest in self-love. And while many single women masturbate regularly, others prefer total celibacy. Both single and partnered women may experience monthly cycles of self-desire.

Some coupled women become upset on discovering that their partner masturbates, fearing that the solo sexuality subtracts from the relationship. But masturbation and partnered sex differ significantly; reasons for occasionally preferring the former include privacy, simplicity, and efficiency. Such needs do not reflect badly on a relationship.

Many couples integrate masturbation into their partnered sex. For instance, women who have trouble coming often prefer to bring themselves to orgasm, even when making love with someone else. One partner masturbating frees the other to play with her breasts or kiss her or penetrate her or some combination thereof. Many women enjoy watching their lover touch herself. Or both partners may masturbate at the same time. It's all fun!

Techniques. Masturbation is a wonderful way to discover your own desires. Do you want to focus totally on your genitals or include full-body foreplay? Do you want a quick orgasm before you fall asleep? Or do you prefer to explore yourself? Do you favor soft strokes or firm ones? Rapid or languid motions? Attention paid to your breasts? Inner thighs? Knees? All of the above? How about music and candlelight? Sexy clothing?

Masturbation is as individual as the person masturbating.

In the most common form of female masturbation, you lie on your back and rub your clitoris with one or two fingers until you come or don't want to masturbate anymore. Try different strokes, pressures, speeds, and angles.

You may enjoy penetrating your vagina with your fingers (or dildo, cucumber, or candle). Explore different rhythms; one exciting approach alternates nine short strokes with one long one. Also investigate different-sized penetrators; vaginal capacities vary widely.

Vibrators offer consistent, strong stimulation and can be used either externally, with pressure directly on or close to the clitoris, or internally, with the vibrator in the vagina. Alice swears by a combination of the two. (Do not put plug-in-the-wall vibrators in your vagina; however, there are special attachments, such as the "G Spotter," that are perfect for penetration. See also *Vibrators.*)

Suzanne used to put a pillow between her legs and rub against it, but now she prefers to use a vibrator. Alice enjoys bathtub stimulation, using either her fingers or water from a shower massage. Gail lies on her belly with a vibrator under her stimulating her clitoris. Some

women can reach orgasm simply by wrapping one leg around the other and squeezing their thighs together rhythmically.

Jessica's masturbation techniques have changed over the years: "When I was ten, my mother got me to learn how to meditate. It was great. I'd have to go in a room, lock the door, and be there by myself for twenty minutes! I did meditate too. Anyway, I used to use objects to masturbate. Pencils were always great — moving them very fast across my clitoris and the area in front of my vagina. As I got older and more inventive, and my body changed, I changed my methods. Sometimes I'll just do my clit, other times I'll just go inside my vagina and come that way. I like to lay on my stomach and masturbate. Something about the position is a turn-on. It feels good too. I'll generally use my finger or fingers on my clit and then usually take one hand around and go inside my vagina with two fingers or three fingers. Or maybe use my dildo."

MEETING PEOPLE. Are you looking for someone to talk to or someone to sleep with or someone to love forever? Do you live near a major city filled with choices or in a more rural area where you fear being the only lesbian for miles?

In much of the United States, there are lesbian (or lesbian and gay) support groups, coming-out groups, bars, athletic leagues, archives, dance clubs, religious groups, and political groups. To find them, look in the phone book under "lesbian," "gay," "lavender," and "women." Examine the free newspapers at alternative bookstores. Few lesbian and gay newspapers actually use the words "lesbian and gay" in their titles, so look for clues such as pink triangles, lambdas, and rainbow flags — or phrases using the word "out." (If the paper features a very hunky man in leather on the cover, it's probably a gay paper.) If your locale lacks a lesbian and gay paper, try women's, leftist, and new-age papers for lists of lesbian and gay meetings. (See also *Hotlines* and the *Resource List.*)

If you have no luck with any of these approaches, consider asking a cabdriver the location of the nearest lesbian bar. Of course, seeking such information from a stranger may be frightening and dangerous, but it often works (however, see *Legal Matters).* Oddly enough, homophobes are frequently also excellent sources of information about gay bars and clubs and hangouts. If you overhear at work that Joe Bigot is organizing a picket line, find out where!

But what if your area simply has no lesbian or gay anything? Check out women's organizations and softball teams. Keep an ear out at work for women who follow the careers of k.d. lang or Martina Navratilova or who see every movie with a female star. The clues can be subtle — and they can also be misleading — so be careful when meeting someone this way. Take your time. Drop your own hints ("So, what did you think of Rita Mae Brown's latest book?"). Particularly if you live or work in a very homophobic area, wait for a definite sign that she means what you think she means before coming out to someone you don't know well. And don't ignore gay men; they can introduce you to other gay people, female and male, and they can be first-class friends and allies.

And, finally, there are always personal ads. (See also *Personal Ads.)*

Once you have figured out how to meet lesbians in general comes the challenge of meeting that certain lesbian in particular.

If you are looking for Ms. Right, take your time and get to know lots of lesbians. Some will make better friends than lovers, and those new friends can introduce you to other women or arrange blind dates. Lydia says, "The last live-in lover I met was on a blind date, which is really weird, because this blind date was arranged by one of my very first lovers, whom I met on a blind date!"

When meeting people, avoid seeming desperate or needy. Just be friendly, and just be yourself. If you've joined an organization, get involved in a project where you can meet people naturally, as when you spend an evening with a group stuffing envelopes or playing pool.

Talking to an individual can be much scarier than joining a group, but most women are just as nervous as you are. Don't worry about having a great first line; many women will be glad you said *anything*. Ask her to dance or what she thinks of a TV show or where she works or when she joined the club you're at. *Anything*. As a backup, carry mints or candy and offer her a piece.

Once the ice is broken, a conversation may start easily. If not, try again with someone else. Rejection hurts, but it's not fatal, and the best cure is to find acceptance elsewhere.

If you are seeking someone solely to have sex with, many of the above approaches will still work. When it comes to inviting her home with you — or inviting yourself to her place — varying levels of frankness all work. There are the standards, such as, "Would you like to come to my place for a drink (cup of coffee, whatever)?" or "You're very attractive and I'd love it if you came home with me." They work. Kathy has had some success with "Wanna fuck?", but only with women she has known for a while. A friend of Alice's got laid regularly by standing in the middle of a bar at closing time and yelling, "Anyone want to go home with me?" However, once she got clean and sober, she never did that again.

If a woman rejects your overtures, your feelings will probably get hurt, but she may be rejecting casual sex rather than you in particular.

Whether you're looking for Ms. Right or Ms. Tonight, remember that your self-worth is not dependent on someone else's "Yes." And if at first you don't succeed, try, try again. (See also *Bars; Dating; Hotlines; Rejection; Symbols.*)

MEN. What are men doing in a book on lesbian sex? Many lesbians have had sex with men, and some still do. And even the most devoted 120 percent lesbian may occasionally find a man slipping into her fantasies.

Switching from men to women. When lesbians who have had sex with men start having sex with women, they tend to be *extremely enthusiastic* about the change. After all, lesbians, being lesbians, desire women more than they desire men. But there are also general differences in sexual styles between most men and most women.

Gail remembers, "With guys, the whole tongue is down your throat. Women are a little more gentle and playful, and the art of following and leading happens more with women. It's not as nice with men; I guess I don't like to be choked." Suzanne says, "With men, foreplay was all the stuff I liked, which they would do a little bit of on the way to what they liked."

When talking about sex with women, newly out lesbians often mention the joy of having choices and the freedom to be aggressive. Also, many women describe their pleasure in discovering that, with other women, they can sometimes just cuddle without having sex.

These changes often allow lesbians to further explore their sexuality: it was with women, after years of experience with men, that Kathy had her first orgasm from oral sex, that Suzanne discovered she was multiorgasmic, and that Rebecca started having vaginal orgasms.

Fantasizing about men. Some lesbians fantasize (rarely, occasionally, or frequently) that they are having sex with men, that they are men having sex with women, that they are men having sex with men, that they are being watched by men, that they are watching men, and so on. Fantasizing about men doesn't make someone less of a lesbian. A fantasy is just that — a fantasy.

Having sex with men after coming out. Even after coming out, some lesbians still enjoy having sex with men. But, you may ask, are they lesbians if they sleep with men? Well, *they* feel they are. Jessica says, "I know women, who call themselves lesbians, who do make love with men sometimes. They'll say, 'I only do it when I just want sex. If I want an emotional connection, forget it.' And sometimes I think, maybe I could do that again. You know, just for the sex."

Many lesbians deny that women who sleep with men are lesbians (while others insist that women who call themselves bisexual are really lesbians who are too scared to come out). The lesbian community encompasses millions of women, and each has an opinion. Each also has the right to live her own life, and identify herself, according to her own beliefs.

But there are ramifications to having sex with men. Birth control is required. For vaginal and anal intercourse, safer sex guidelines must be followed. And some lesbians simply will not have sex with women who sleep with men. Period. (See also *Bisexuality; Heterosexuality Survivors; HIV; Safer Sex.*)

MENOPAUSE. Menopause does not always occur as a natural part of the aging cycle. Various cancer therapies cause instant menopause (also referred to as *chemical menopause),* which shares many symptoms with organic menopause. With both forms, menstruation ceases, and moodiness and hot flashes may occur. The menopause experience can be erratic, as occasionally menstruation reappears, and depressions show up and leave on their own timetable. However, not all women feel these negative effects from menopause.

Lydia finds starting menopause to be emotionally trying: "I feel resistant, real resistant. My image of myself is being very young — in both negative and positive ways. In terms of sex, I'm finding more vaginal dryness, which pisses me off. I'm noticing some changes in my body, in the texture of my skin. I'm getting more hair where I don't want hair. I'm getting a beard. I don't like it. I've had to switch to smaller dildos because of changes in my vagina. And because I'm drier, being fisted has become a problem."

Menopause is frequently accompanied by the reduced vaginal lubrication Lydia mentions, as well as thinning of the vaginal walls. In addition, some women experience diminution of sexual desire during and after menopause. These symptoms may pass as their bodies adjust to new hormonal balances, and sexual desire may return. Rebecca, who went through chemical menopause some ten years ago, and who suffered years of vaginal dryness, has started getting wet again; in addition, she says sex with her new lover is the most exciting she's had in years.

It is always possible, if annoying, to adapt to physical changes. A woman may grieve the loss of natural lubrication but still be grateful for commercial lubricants. Similarly, while changes in vaginal texture may lessen the ability to enjoy vigorous sex, less energetic forms of stimulation may become *more* erotic. However, before adapting to these transitions, it is probably necessary, and certainly healthy, to deal with personal grief and anger at aging and body changes.

If your sexual desire doesn't return on its own, you can explore new ways to get in the mood. Changing habits may help. Add erotica or more foreplay — or eliminate foreplay entirely. Keep sex a frequent part of your life; the longer you go without, the harder it is to start up again. Try new forms of masturbation to discover the new, post-menopausal, you. Be open to redefinitions of sex; nongenital stimulation may become more exciting as genital stimulation becomes less — or vice versa.

Perhaps the most important way to stay sexual is to decide to have sex just because you want to, even if that "want" feels more theoretical than physical. Make a date with your partner or yourself to have some romantic body time, but with no expectations. It may take a while, measured in hours, days, even months, before you experience feelings you would call sexual; until then, let yourself fully enjoy cuddling and stroking and other sensations *as they feel now*. Don't keep searching for your old responses; welcome your new ones.

If none of these approaches work for you, consider whether your sexual reluctance is masking other problems. Perhaps you are bored in your relationship; perhaps past abuse issues are bothering you. Therapy may be in order.

It is also possible that you will decide that you just don't care to be sexual anymore.

For more information on menopause, see the book *Ourselves, Growing Older*, Gail Sheehy's *The Silent Passage*, and Germaine Greer's *The Change*.

MENSTRUATION. Women vary in their comfort around having sex during menstruation. Jenn doesn't like to have somebody go down on her while she has her period. For Gail, it's no problem. Suzanne says, "It depends on how heavy the flow is. Toward the end of the period, penetration and some dirty fingers are fine. With heavy, heavy flow, penetration doesn't seem too exciting. Oral sex with a tampon in is fine." Jessica enjoys sex during her period, but she says, "I've never gone down on somebody who had their period — it just hasn't happened. I would be scared of the transmission likelihood of AIDS being higher." (See also *AIDS*.)

Some women find menstruation to be a period of heightened sexuality. Suzanne explains, "I'm really, really horny right before I start my period and during my period, and I really want penetration." Others find their sexual desire lost in cramps, aches, and bloatedness.

Orgasms are reputed to be good for cramps. But are they? Suzanne says, "I've discovered that, as a delayed reaction, orgasms are also bad for cramps. I think immediately after orgasm, cramps do feel better, maybe because you're suffused with glee. But sometimes the uterine contractions can ultimately make cramps worse." Kathy says, "Cramps after orgasms ease at first, then they hurt worse for a while, and then they feel better. It's worth the achy part for the relaxation that follows." Jenn says simply, "I do find sex and orgasms to be good for my cramps."

Obviously, each woman's cramps respond uniquely to orgasms. If you've never tried it, masturbate the next time you have your period — you know, for medicinal reasons only.

MIRRORS. Watching yourself in a mirror while masturbating can be a great turn-on. Savor your every move as you enjoy your own breasts and belly and thighs. Or you and a partner can view your sex play from brand-new angles as you make love.

But for women who aren't comfortable with their bodies, mirrors can be frightening or discomforting. As Jenn says, "It's enough that I hear myself; I don't want to see myself too. I don't want to be looking at me. I want to look at her." Suzanne feels the same way: "It's been weird having mirrored closet doors. That's a new dimension. Certain things I can look at in the mirror and like. Us together or my breasts. But I can't look at my belly and thighs."

Even when both partners feel good about their bodies, mirrors may induce a level of self-consciousness that inhibits sex. One woman said she became more focused on how she looked than how she felt.

MONEY. For some people, money equals sex as a source of anxiety. Are you okay if you make too little? Are you okay if you make too much? What *is* too little or too much? If you go on a date, who pays? When you live together, should you share expenses? If one woman pays more of the bills, is the other a lesser partner? Should you get a joint checking account?

There are no set answers to these questions. People from different ethnic groups, different classes, and different families deal with money in different ways. While one woman may share money easily, another will be reluctant to even talk about it. Some people consider money a means to an end, and others gauge a person's worth by how much she earns.

Money differences between two women can best be solved through communication and compromise — if they're solvable. Money conversations must be totally honest, even if they are uncomfortable. For instance, if you resent her inability to pay half of the rent, say so, or your resentment will show up elsewhere, like in your sex life or in an argument about what to watch on TV. (Also keep in mind that your methods for dealing with money may evolve during the course of a relationship. For instance, you may decide not to pool your money until you've been together a few years.)

When you do come to a comfortable agreement about how to deal with money, consider keeping it to yourselves. Otherwise, people outside your relationship may be too willing to criticize your choices. If you share money, you may get chided for not being individuals. If one of you supports the other, you are almost certain to be called *codependent*. And if you keep your money absolutely separate, you may be accused of lack of commitment. Don't listen. It's no one's business but your own.

If you want to leave your money to your lover, make sure you write out a will or set up a trust; no matter how long you two are together, as a same-gender couple you have no legal connection in the eyes of the law. (See also *Legal Matters.*)

MONOGAMY. Monogamy is not required. This simple fact shocks some people, since society teaches from childhood that eternal faithfulness to one partner is superior to all other types of relationships. However, many species of animals do not practice monogamy, and there are no absolute reasons for people to stick with one partner.

Historically, monogamy took root in humans as a way to guarantee that a woman only had kids by her husband; this made father-to-son legacies possible. Lesbian relationships, however, have no need to guarantee male inheritance lines.

Nevertheless, most lesbians choose monogamy. If their first monogamous relationship isn't a success, they get into a second one.

And if that isn't a success, they try a third. This is known as "serial monogamy." Some women eventually settle with one partner, while others continue their string of monogamous relationships.

This pattern works well for many people; nevertheless, it is not required. If you have never considered other options, you might want to examine what *you* seek in a relationship before making a commitment. If you discover that you don't know what you want, a period of dating can help you find out.

Nonmonogamy is a challenge, often stirring up jealousy and insecurity; the nonmonogamous woman may occasionally yearn for the stability of a long-term relationship. However, monogamy is also a challenge, requiring two people to get along and somehow stay fresh and romantic year after year; the monogamous woman may occasionally yearn for unpredictable sex with someone new.

If you do choose monogamy, you can enjoy what San Diego psychologist Sharon Young refers to as "the freedom of commitment." You don't have to keep one foot out the door. You don't have to constantly wonder, "Is she right for me?" You don't have to care what your parents and friends think. You can survive bad times *because you choose to.* It's a liberating form of commitment.

Whatever lifestyle you choose, you owe no apologies to anyone. You only live once (at least in this particular incarnation), and you have the right to live the life you desire.

MOTHERHOOD. See *Children.*

MULTIPLE ORGASMS. Many women experience multiple orgasms, and they love them; others are quite pleased with just one. In *The Hite Report*, roughly 50 percent of the women surveyed found single orgasms to be sufficient.

The period between multiple orgasms varies from woman to woman. Jenn says her clit needs to rest a couple of minutes, and then she can just come and come and come. For Jessica, "Number two is just a few seconds away. I've had up to five with one person; by myself I can have seven." Jessica also experiences what she calls "aftershocks": "I'll have an orgasm and it will kind of end and then there will be these little echoes of it."

How much time must pass between orgasms before they become totally separate rather than parts of one multi? That's in the eye of the beholder, and it probably has more to do with labeling than with sex.

Some previously uniorgasmic women have, over time, developed the ability to achieve multiple orgasms. Suzanne says, "I wasn't multiorgasmic until I was with women. I never thought about working on it. Then I was with a multiorgasmic woman. At first I thought it was kind of a pain in the butt because she kept wanting more and more and more. But knowing that it was possible — I guess I just needed to learn about it rather than 'work' on it — I had to learn what the rhythms were. I found I didn't want to be touched right on the clit immediately after I came. There was a sort of episodic nature to it."

Alice says, "When I used to just have one orgasm, it was bigger. Now that I have multis, each is smaller. Sometimes it feels like one long orgasm being continued. It's fun no matter how it happens."

If you desire more orgasms, you can practice by yourself or with a partner. Experiment with maintaining a light motionless touch on the clitoris after the first orgasm, then gradually add movement. Or try leaving the clit alone for a minute or two, then stimulate it gently. Switching the type of arousal may help: use a vibrator for the first orgasm and a tongue for the second; or tongue for the first, fingers for the second; or vaginal for the first, clitoral for the second. If your level of arousal lessens after the first orgasm, add erotica or more foreplay for the second.

Listen to your body; she will tell you what to do. However, it is possible that her message will be "one is enough." (See also *Kegel Exercises.*)

MUSH. (Sweet talk.)

Few lesbians are ambivalent about mush; we either love it or hate it. Some couples evolve an entire intimate language of mush. As Suzanne said when discussing the words she and her lover use for sex: "There's a sort of baby-talk vocabulary we use too." Kathy and her lover have invented a pseudo-romance language of mush that would make a linguist tear her hair.

It's rare that a couple's sweet personal language is even bearable to the outside listener. And that's what's so wonderful: mush is absolutely personal.

Even if you can't stand "sweet-ums" and "honey-bunny-hon," don't give up on all love talk. In a relationship, the adult daily minimum mush requirement is at least one "I love you," and even the most casual sex is enriched by compliments and expressions of pleasure.

MUTUAL MASTURBATION. (Simultaneously touching each other's clitorises, often to orgasm.)

When touching someone else's clitoris, experiment with all the techniques you've learned from masturbating, keeping in mind that women differ in what they like. Start gently, as it may take a while for your partner to adjust to your touch. Extra lubrication always helps, as does communication. Ask your partner what she enjoys; perhaps she prefers to be touched through her labia, or maybe the left side of

her clit is more sensitive than the right. With time and sensitivity, you will learn each other's preferences and rhythms.

One glory of mutual masturbation (MM), besides the excitement of concurrently touching and being touched, is the wealth of intimate positions possible. You can lie on your sides facing each other, or sit cross-legged facing each other, or lie on your backs side by side, or sit next to each other, or stand up together. Many of these positions allow kissing, hugging, stroking, and pressing your breasts together as well as MM.

For outdoor sex with minimum undressing, MM can be done with your hands in each other's pants or up each other's skirt. If you have the requisite anatomy and sensitivity, MM can also be accomplished through your clothing.

Although MM can lead to simultaneous orgasms, for many women, it is an end in itself. As discussed under *Simultaneous Orgasms,* striving to come at the same time can be tiring, intimidating, and distracting — but if simultaneous Os are what you want, MM is a great technique.

MYTHS. A terrible obstacle to coming out gracefully is the antilesbian myths that lesbians hear, and internalize, as we are growing up. But myths are just that: myths. Not the truth. For instance:

Lesbians are child molesters. Study after study has shown that lesbians rarely molest children and that most child molesters are heterosexual men.

Lesbians will sleep with any women. The legend of the sexually voracious lesbian must spring from the imaginations of nervous heterosexuals, since it certainly doesn't come from reality. When lesbians and other groups are compared, lesbians always have the fewest past lovers. We absolutely know how to say "no" — as a matter of fact, lesbian humor often refers to a lack of ability to say "yes"! Lesbians do not simply grab and attack the nearest female passing by.

Interestingly enough, many lesbians have found that the straight women who most fear their advances are the last ones on earth the lesbians would actually want to sleep with.

Lesbians are ugly. This myth has its roots in two misconceptions: (1) that butch women are ugly, and (2) that all lesbians are butch. With TV and movies constantly displaying hyper-"feminine" women with slinky clothing, too much makeup, and 0 percent body fat, it is not surprising that butch women strike the ignorant or untutored eye as ugly. But, breaking away from the ingrained stereotypes of contemporary attractiveness, it's easy to see just how beautiful butch women are, with their handsome faces, strong bodies, and often stylish *(butch stylish, not mainstream stylish)* clothing.

Ignorant people believe that all lesbians are butch because it is only butch women whom they recognize as lesbians. The same people might look right past feminine lesbians, assuming them to be straight. But there are many feminine lesbians, and stunning ones at that.

Kathy recalls the awe of a newly out lesbian on seeing her first gorgeous gay woman: "She kept asking, 'Are you sure she's a lesbian? Are you *sure?*' She was so well trained that she just couldn't accept this woman's beauty. I finally told her, 'Yes, she's really a lesbian. And you should see her lover!'"

Lesbians can't get men. Most of us have had men. We just don't want them.

Lesbians got "that way" because they were raped. This is the saddest myth, since an unfortunately high percentage of lesbians have indeed been raped or molested or incested. But so have an unfortunately high percentage of straight women. If rape caused lesbianism, more than 30 percent of women would be gay!

Recent studies have shown some evidence that homosexuality in men results from biological forces rather than from conditioning or childhood experiences. Whether these studies hold up and whether they are relevant to women remains to be seen.

NIBBLING. Nibbling and biting thrill many women. Gentle nibbles tend to be more appropriate in early foreplay, while harder bites feel better later on. With arousal comes a heightened resistance to pain, and bites that would usually be uncomfortable become sexy.

Enthusiastic biting can leave marks, so be careful. If your lover has an important business meeting the next day, she probably won't relish a huge hickey on her neck — though she might cherish a little one in a more discreet location as a reminder of your evening together.

Some women enjoy being bitten very hard; however, intense biting is not wise if either or both partners are drunk or stoned, as inebriation raises pain tolerance and lessens judgment, always a dangerous combination.

NONMONOGAMY. See *Monogamy.*

NUDITY. There are many ways to get undressed. Sometimes neither of you can wait to shuck your clothes; other times, slow and sexy stripping is in order. Long-term couples occasionally fall into a pattern of quickly undressing when they know they're going to have sex; the occasional evening that breaks the pattern will add spice to their lives.

Of course, total nudity is not required for good sex. Some women prefer being partially clothed as a turn-on; incest survivors, women who have had mastectomies, and other women who experience discomfort with their bodies may sometimes feel safer and more comfortable with some clothing on. Or a couple may choose to keep some clothing on just for a change of pace.

NUMBERS. Do lesbians have many sexual partners? It depends on the individual and how you define *many*.

The Gay Report related that approximately 62 percent of the lesbians surveyed had had one to ten lovers in their lives, and 35 percent had had eleven to fifty. *Homosexualities* reported similar numbers: approximately 58 percent of lesbians had had fewer than ten lovers, and approximately 33 percent had had between ten and fifty. Unfortunately, these findings are from the 1970s, and there is no way to know if they have changed or how accurately they reflected the general lesbian community in the first place. (See also *Statistics*.)

Some lesbians have had sex with only one woman (or none) and others have had sex with hundreds. Based on highly anecdotal evidence, the average seems to be approximately two lovers per year of active lesbianism. This doesn't mean each lesbian sleeps with two women each year; more often, a woman is monogamous for years, goes through a breakup, enjoys a flurry of activity, then becomes monogamous again.

O

ONE-NIGHT STANDS. See *Casual Sex.*

ORAL SEX. (Licking or sucking the clitoris, labia, or vagina, often to orgasm; also known as "going down on." Note: most of the techniques in this section can work with or without a dental dam. See *Safer Sex.*)

So you've finally wended your way between her legs. Now what do you do?

That depends on you and on her.

One typical approach includes kissing her pubic hair, with special attention paid to the seam of labia right down the middle. On some women, the labia will be prominent and accessible; on others, they will be buried under tangled pubic hair. To gain access to her more hidden parts, you can lick along that seam of labia until she opens up, separate her labia with your fingers, or ask her to open her lips for you. Each way offers its own erotic thrill.

Once her lips have been opened, you will be facing a picture somewhat like that in the *Anatomy* entry. If the lights are on, you may see glistening pink, red, brown, or purplish flesh, with a shape resembling a flower. (After you've had oral sex a few times with the lights on, you will never look at a Georgia O'Keeffe painting the same way again!)

At the top of her vulva, where her inner lips meet, is her clitoris. Depending on her personal architecture, it might be readily visible or somewhat hidden. A simple way to find it is to lick up the length of her vulva; when you reach a little knob, you're there. (Her clitoris may be the size of a grain of rice or of a fingertip, or anywhere in between.) Her moans of pleasure will affirm that you are at the right place. And if you're not sure, ask!

Of course, you're not required to go directly to her clit. There are all sorts of things you might want to try first.

For instance, gently blow (or puff) air onto her whole vulval area. A focused stream will feel different to her than a more diffuse one, but both are likely to feel good. If you are put off by her smell (that does happen sometimes), blowing on her is a sexy way to lessen that smell.

Don't ignore her labia. Lick or suck them, or nibble them very tenderly. Some women like stronger labial stimulation; make sure she is one of them before getting too energetic. Build the stimulation gradually.

Many women find it thrilling to be penetrated by their lover's tongue. This may not be the easiest thing to do, depending on the length and flexibility of your tongue and the size and shape of her vulva. Sometimes changing angles helps; if she's lying on her back, put a pillow under her hips so that her vagina is more accessible, then thrust your tongue in and out, or lick around the vaginal opening. (Warning from Kathy: "I've licked so deep into my lover that I've injured that little web under my tongue that holds it to the bottom of my mouth. But it was worth it!")

You can use your tongue to stroke her slowly from her vagina to her clit. A more rapid version of the same stroke also works. Use the point of your tongue, or try wide flat strokes. The pressure can be hard, medium, or teasingly soft. Occasionally, soft strokes will tickle her unpleasantly; in that case, be more firm. Little by little, work your way to her clit — or else visit it occasionally, lick elsewhere, and go back, again and again.

Once you're ready to focus on her clit, and perhaps bring her to orgasm, you have countless options. Whatever approach you choose, a usually reliable rule of tongue is to start gently and slowly, then gradually get quicker or firmer — or both.

Try various approaches at various speeds and pressures, and note how she responds. Lick circles around her clit. Suck it gently or harder, as seems appropriate. Lick it directly or through her labia. Kiss it with soft wet lips. (Be careful to keep your teeth out of the way unless you *know* that's something she likes.) Try humming while she's in your mouth, to add a sort of vibrator effect.

One lovely stroke involves putting your entire tongue flat against her vulva, inside her labia, and slowly, slowly, almost imperceptibly, dragging it up along her clit. It may take a full minute for this stroke to be completed, during which her sensation builds subtly and steadily.

Whatever strokes you try, don't jump around too much from one to the other. Try subtle segues; finesse and grace count. But don't drive yourself crazy with performance anxiety; it takes a bit of time to learn what a woman likes sexually, and there's no reason you should be able to read her mind.

If she doesn't make sex noises or move much, that doesn't necessarily mean she's not enjoying herself. Some women are just quiet. Pay attention to the movement of her hips and the tension in her thighs, which can be revealing. And if you feel totally lost, ask what she likes.

The key to pleasing some women is not just the oral sex itself but what you add to it. Gail says, "If my lover is giving me oral sex with a hand on my boob and another hand in my mouth, *that* is total heaven."

As your partner grows more excited and seems to near orgasm, stick to one or two strokes that clearly please her. The closer she gets, the more she will desire steady and reliable stimulation. Once she seems very near, stick to whatever stroke you're using until she comes. (You can tell she's getting closer to orgasm through various cues: She may moan more, or more loudly, or more deeply. She may clench her hands or tense her pelvic area. Her breath will come more rapidly. She may thrash around a bit. Generally, she will exhibit a buildup of physical tension.)

Different women prefer different speeds of stimulation to come. Some women need to be licked faster and faster, while others can come to a moderate, steady tempo. The faster approach often makes a woman come more explosively, while the slower tempo may cause a different sort of orgasm to unfold. However, keep in mind that, once they are nearing orgasm, some women are frustrated by slower licking. On the other hand, some women find hard and fast licking over-stimulating, and they may need to calm down a bit to come.

Again, don't worry about doing everything perfectly; it takes time to learn a particular woman's needs and desires. No reasonable woman will expect you to know exactly the best way to make her come the first time around.

Some women take longer to come than others. If you start to get tired, which you might, think of ways to keep up the stimulation without exhausting yourself. For instance, if you are licking her in circles around her clit, you can switch between making the circles with your tongue and making them by moving your head with your tongue loosely pointed; this gives some muscles a rest while others work. Interspersing wet, wet clit kisses with licking will also help.

If necessary, switch to touching her with your fingers. Do this as subtly as possible. You can slip your finger into your mouth and touch her with a very wet finger while your mouth is still against her.

And you can always ask her to take over. Alice says, "Sometimes my jaw goes out and I have to ask my lover to bring herself to orgasm. I stroke her and kiss her while she comes. It works out fine." Whether you're new to each other or a long-term couple, it helps if you and your partner have good communication.

A nice dessert offering, as she's coming, is to merge your licking into sucking, then hold a soft steady suck with your tongue motionless against her clit. This can make her orgasm feel longer and more intense. Stay still for a while, then either move your tongue away, or start working on Orgasm 2, The Sequel.

If you decide to try to make her come again, give her a bit of time to calm down from the first orgasm. Then start licking again, very gently, and see how she reacts. If she is clearly aroused, keep going and she may have more orgasms. If she is not multiorgasmic or she just doesn't want more stimulation, she can stop you by moving away, inviting you to come hold her, or just saying, "Thanks, that's all I need."

While it's useful to have experience and technical knowledge when doing oral sex, the most important factor is to enjoy yourself. Because of past training that female genitalia are ugly (or smell like fish!), it may take a while to relax and savor going down on a woman. Some women never do get into it, but many find it one of the best ways to spend time on earth.

Take your time; discover what you really enjoy. You can learn as you go. Luxuriate in her taste and smell. Enjoy giving her pleasure. And feel your own pleasure as well! If you truly, wholeheartedly, love licking her, she'll find that the biggest turn-on of all.

ORGASMS. According to *The New Our Bodies, Ourselves,* "Orgasm is the point at which [body] tension is suddenly released in a series of involuntary and pleasurable muscular contractions which expel blood from the pelvic tissues." In an article called "Evolution of the Big O" (*Discover* magazine), writer Karen Wright calls orgasm a "pudendal cataclysm [that] typically lasts less than a minute." JoAnn Loulan writes in *Lesbian Sex* that orgasm "is a spasmodic response to the extreme engorgement of the pelvic region. From three to fifteen contractions occur, 4/5 of a second apart, releasing the fluid and blood from the engorged tissues." She adds, "No one wants a muscle spasm in her leg, but everyone wants one between her legs."

For some women, reaching orgasm is the point of having sex; for others, it is the icing on the cake. But what does an orgasm *feel* like?

To Lydia, "it feels like going up the crest of a roller coaster and getting closer and closer and closer to the top and then going down." Jenn says, "It's like a rumbling that starts in your toes. A rush. I just quiver and shake and everything moves and moans. I love it."

For Suzanne, "it's like climbing a mountain. There's different ways to get to the top, and different things happen when you get there. Sometimes, it's kind of a lip and you just spill over it. Other times, it is more explosive. I love the time right before an orgasm, so there's part of me that wants to just stay there — and another part of me is going, yahoo! — over we go! Sometimes, I can feel myself almost flying into it. I like also the throbby aftereffects."

For Gail, orgasm "involves my stomach muscles and my breathing — I mainly feel it from my vagina up. It's a mental thing, too." And Rebecca says, "There are different kinds of orgasms. Some go up into my head. I feel like I just explode up. Then there's a kind that goes down my legs, and that's marvelous. And then there are vaginal orgasms, which involve the whole body with this tremendous buildup and then a release of tension. It feels like going up, up, up, up, up, up, up, and then exploding."

For Jessica, "an orgasm is an extreme gathering of energy and power. It's a crescendo. You can come with just your genitals or you can come with your entire body. And with your mind too. It's a rush, like a very intense tingle. I get really hot and sweaty, and sometimes I get just totally drenched."

No wonder people crave orgasms. But not everyone finds her orgasmic response so satisfying. Kathy says, "I sometimes have little nothing orgasms, and they really disappoint me. I also get jealous of women who are multiorgasmic." For Alice, "coming is nice, but it's not my favorite part of sex. I'll take getting penetrated over having an orgasm any day."

Knowledge about female orgasm is limited, and biologists still argue over the reproductive and evolutionary "adaptive value" of a woman coming. Luckily, lesbian sexuality occurs largely out of the reproductive loop, and orgasms lacking "adaptive value" feel just as good as orgasms that continue the species.

Another controversy among sex researchers and scientists is whether or not vaginal orgasms exist. However, the women interviewed for this book experienced not only vaginal orgasms, but also anal orgasms and breast orgasms! One woman had an orgasm watching the famous "butter scene" in *Last Tango in Paris*.

Whatever the biological and evolutionary root of orgasms, and whether they come from the clitoris, vagina, or movie screen, orgasms offer sheer pleasure. When life gets tense, coming can be like taking a small vacation. And sharing orgasms with a lover is one of life's true gifts.

If you've never had an orgasm or would like to improve the orgasms you have, see *Masturbation* and *Sexual Growth*.

OUTDOOR SEX. Imagine making love on a beautiful deserted beach on a hot midsummer's day. The sky floats above like a perfect blue canopy. The waves splash in and out to the rhythm of your movements. The sun bathes you and your lover in a blanket of natural warmth. Sex has never felt so right, so natural.

Lovely, huh?

Now imagine sand in your ears and in your crotch. A lifeguard comes biking down the sand and you manage to cover yourselves just before he passes by; then you realize that the feeling of heat on your skin wasn't just sexual — you've gotten a bad sunburn.

The beauty of outdoor sex is that it happens outdoors. The problem with outdoor sex is that it happens outdoors. But everyone seems to try it at least once. Jenn managed a bit of privacy by parking her station wagon in a deserted area with the hatchback open to let in the "starlight, fresh breeze, and all this space." She also once got away with discreetly masturbating her lover on a crowded San Francisco trolley. Lydia, on the other hand, got caught with her pants down in the woods.

If you want to try outdoor sex, women's music festivals offer a safe arena. Elsewhere, consider bringing along friends to protect you while you have fun. Avoid total nudity unless you have a bathrobe or something you can put on *quickly*, and watch out for insects and animals, both four-legged and two-legged. Beware of states with tough sodomy laws; the same behavior that would get a straight couple a tsk-tsk and a wink from a cop might get a lesbian couple arrested. (See also *Legal Matters.)*

Despite all the caveats, outdoor sex has its appeal, and even the negatives can turn into positives. As Kathy relates, "I was fucking my then-lover Pat on a blanket under some pine trees when ants started to crawl on my hand. Pat was really into it, and I hated to interrupt her pleasure, so I added a sort of jolt to my strokes to knock the ants off. Not only did I succeed in getting rid of the insects, but I also discovered a whole new stroke that Pat *loved."*

P

PENETRATION. (Going inside a woman's vagina or anus with fingers or dildo; also known as fucking.)

Despite the heterosexual model on which we were all raised, penetration is not a required part of sex, and some women practice it rarely, if at all. When penetration does occur in lesbian sex, it generally (though not always) follows a fair amount of foreplay, including stroking, kissing, rubbing, touching, and oral sex (though some women prefer oral sex *after* penetration and others skip oral sex entirely).

The following discussion focuses on vaginal penetration with fingers from the point of view of the penetrator. For your partner's safety, make sure your nails are short and well filed before starting.

You and your partner have been messing around, and you're both turned on. You reach between her legs and stroke her. After a few caresses, her vulva unfolds and you discover that she is swollen, hot, and wet. (If she is not, you can always use a lubricant.) You resist swooning and continue stroking her. At the base of her vulva, toward her anus, you slip one finger into her vagina. (If you cannot find it, if you are nervous, or if you are shy, ask her to guide you in.) If she says she is uncomfortable with penetration, gently remove your finger and ask what she likes. She may want to continue the penetration, but at her own speed, or she may ask to switch to something else.

Assume all systems are go and you've got one finger inside her now. It may fit snugly or it may be lost in a relatively large space. If so, add another finger or two. In later lovemaking sessions you might *start* penetration with three or four fingers, but early on, take the time to learn her preferences. Also, since capacities can change with different levels of arousal and at different points in the menstrual cycle, she may want you to use more or fewer fingers at other times. (If she is wildly bucking up against your hand, go for it! The information a woman's body gives you always supersedes the information a book gives you.)

Once you are inside, start exploring. You can move your fingers gently in and out just the slightest bit or use long slow strokes. Or vary quick short strokes with occasional long ones. Twisting your fingers will give her one sensation and bending them will give her another. Some women prefer that you not move your fingers at all.

Angles are important in penetration. If she is on her back and you're penetrating her palm-up, try moving your fingers in and out in a straight line toward the back of her vagina. Then switch to a long stroke with fingers bent and tilted so that you are hitting the top wall of her vagina (imagine you're aiming at the middle of her pubic hair). You may find that her excitement takes a quantum leap with this angle. Vary which part of the vaginal wall you stimulate; some women are more sensitive toward the opening, while others are more sensitive toward their uterus. Be careful of bumping into her cervix; some women find that sexy; for others, it's painful.

When you find the part of her vaginal wall that is most sensitive, chances are that you are at her G-spot, but don't worry about its name. Just keep trying different ways of stimulating her there; rub, drag, tap, stroke, and hit it with your fingertips. (The word *hit* may sound harsh, but many women adore the sensation. For instance, Suzanne says, "I love being made love to hard.")

The timing of penetration can be tricky. Some women prefer a gradual buildup of intensity and speed, while others adore flurries of serious fucking separated by periods of quiet internal stroking. Follow her body's instructions, and, if you're not sure, ask. Under these circumstances, a gasped "Faster?" or "Harder?" or "Softer?" is plenty of communication.

While penetrating her, try rubbing or massaging her uterus, ovaries, belly, or pubic area with your other hand. This doesn't work for everyone, but it sends some women to another planet.

What happens if you get tired? You're human. But there are ways of going longer. Alternately rely on different muscle groups; for instance, move your fingers alone for a while, and then switch to moving your hand and lower arm together. Or keep your arm and fingers loose and move the whole unit from your shoulders. Occasionally adjust your body's position to vary the pressures on it. And don't underestimate the strength of your imagination; Alice says, "If my lover is just about to come and my arm is dying, I make believe I'm in the Olympics and I need to hold on just a little longer to get a gold medal."

(Ah, yes, vaginal orgasms. They either exist or they don't; see *Vaginal Orgasms.*)

Penetration plus! The crème de la crème of sex for many women is penetration *plus*. The "plus" may be anal sex or oral sex or oral sex with belly rubbing or oral sex with breast kneading or anal sex *and* oral sex or whatever wondrous combo you can invent and perform.

These combinations take skill, coordination, and confidence; don't expect to pull them off the first time you make love to a woman. (However, if you do, more power to you!) Gain experience in oral sex and in penetration before you combine the two, otherwise you may feel like you're rubbing your belly and patting the top of your head at the same time.

Attempting a combo can be as simple as adding another sexual component to what you are already doing. But it also helps to think ahead. If you're going to add breast stimulation, make sure your arm doesn't end up under her thigh. To rub her belly, you need an angle that allows you some downward pressure. For extra penetration, you need a lubricant nearby.

A fiercely fun threesome includes oral sex, vaginal penetration, and anal penetration. In one possible scenario, you start by licking her. As she grows more aroused, you add vaginal penetration and, then, a finger or two in her anus. (Or you can penetrate her anally first; the order doesn't much matter.) Once your finger is in her anus, you can pretty much ignore it, as the movement of you penetrating her vagina plus her hips rocking will be enough to stimulate her anally. Concentrate on the vaginal penetration and oral sex, which are plenty to keep your attention!

This approach may take some planning — or some assistance from your partner — since you will need plenty of lubrication for both her vagina and anus. And you must make sure, as always, never to let anything that has touched her anus near her vagina. If you lose track of what's been where, stop what you're doing and wash your hands (or the dildo or her vulva or all of the above) thoroughly. It may be frustrating to interrupt the festivities, but it's better than giving her an infection.

A simpler but less flexible way to accomplish multi-penetration utilizes one hand. Put your thumb in her vagina and your first finger in her anus; this is particularly effective if she doesn't prefer copious vaginal penetration. You'll have a hand free, which is an advantage, but the thumb in the vagina is not as flexible as a few fingers, which is a disadvantage. (If she *does* prefer more vaginal penetration, you can put your thumb in her anus and your fingers in her vagina; however, this position may strain your wrist, unless she's lying on her belly.) If attempting a combo sounds daunting, involve your lover in the planning. Tell her, "I've got something special I want to do tonight, but I need your help." Then get out the lubricant. Try different positions and angles. See where she likes to be rubbed while being penetrated. Ask for suggestions. Experimentation can be incredibly sexy if you treat it as foreplay rather than merely mechanics. (See also *Anal Sex; Dildos; G-Spot.*)

PERFUMES. See *Scents.*

PERSONAL ADS. If you live in an area with few lesbians, if you seek a partner with particular sexual habits, if you're new to town and want to make friends, or if you're looking for a change of pace, consider publishing or answering a personal ad.

Where. Most lesbian and gay newspapers print such ads, as do some national publications, such as *On Our Backs*. In some metropolitan areas, alternative weeklies publish same-gender personal ads, and even the occasional mainstream daily, such as the *Los Angeles Times*, accepts them.

To find the right place for your ad, read the personals in various publications before submitting your own. For instance, *On Our Backs* specializes in frankly hard-core sex ads.

If none of your local publications accepts explicitly lesbian personal ads, look under headings such as "seeking friends." With a little decoding of terms, you may find a "lesbian seeking lover" hidden in with the others. For instance, if she writes "seeking friend to discuss books with; favorite authors include Rita Mae Brown, Katherine Forrest, and Jane Rule," the odds of her being gay are very high. Some clues are more ambiguous ("favorite authors include Emily Dickinson, Virginia Woolf, and Marge Piercy"), and you may need to drop her a line with your own hints before deciding for sure if she's a lesbian.

What to write. Should you choose to write your own ad, first read the ads already printed in your publication of choice. If, for instance, the rest of the ads are very sexual and you seek only friendship, be very specific on that point; otherwise, readers will assume that you, too, seek sex. Also be very specific whether you are seeking "rebellious bottom, into whipping and handcuffs" or "loving partner for gentle long-term relationship."

Many people exaggerate when they write personal ads (or else there are far more "beautiful, intelligent, charming" people than ever seemed possible). Do present yourself in your best light, but don't lie. After all, when you meet, she will see that your brown hair hasn't been blonde in years. Why disappoint a women who's into blondes when you can please a woman who loves brunettes?

A topic of some controversy is whether racial and size preferences should be included in personal ads. After all, an ad saying, "wanted: slim white woman who can pass for straight" may insult heavy women, women of color, and dyky women. On the other hand, the ad honestly denotes who is wanted. This dilemma needs to be solved according to each woman's conscience, but keep in mind two points: (1) you can be specific without being offensive: compare "lady-like woman preferred" with "no dykes!" and (2) by limiting your horizons, you may deprive yourself of a delightful lover. Kathy's lover explains, "I thought I was looking for someone smaller than me, until I met Kathy. Now I'm just thrilled with Kathy's large round body."

PETS. (Also known as "companion animals.")

If indeed reincarnation and transmogrification exist, then we should all pray to come back in our next lives as cats in lesbian households. Lesbians take their pets seriously, lavishing love and attention on them. Alice says, "I once spent an evening with a bunch of lesbians who didn't know each other, and we were uncomfortable until we began discussing our cats. That's all we talked about all night! How cute they were, their illnesses, their interactions, their intelligence. I expected us to pass around baby pictures and brag when 'our kids' got into Harvard."

Unfortunately, a fair number of lesbians are allergic to cats, and their social lives are therefore often restricted. Some lesbians actually hate cats, and theirs is a lonely row to hoe in lesbian-land. And, yes, some lesbians do have dogs, rabbits, snakes, and even pigs — but cats seem to be the lesbian national animal.

What do cats have to do with sex? For one thing, they love to climb on their mistresses while we're "doing it." Kathy says, "Our cat likes to rub against our heads while we're kissing or lie on our backs when we're going down on each other. We usually just lock her out of the room, but, sometimes, we forget. Then, if we're going at it and she jumps on the bed, we're too involved with what we're doing to kick her out. She loves that. She purrs the whole time."

Couples have split over how pets should be treated. One pair parted when one lover insisted the cat be locked out of the house at night; the other lover found the first one cruel for banishing her feline buddy. (See also *Manners.*)

POLITICAL CORRECTNESS. (Adherence to certain beliefs, largely based on a strict interpretation of feminism or lesbian separatism.)

Initially, the term *politically correct* tweaked people who took their politics so seriously that they lost their senses of humor. As time passed, some lesbians embraced the term as an expression of the desire to be feminist, nonracist, nonableist, and generally inclusive and fair. The far right then appropriated the term to label anyone believing in equal rights as some sort of anti-Freedom of Speech liberal fascist.

In the context of lesbian sex, political correctness tends to censure any form of sexuality that could be interpreted as "male-identified" or "reflecting the patriarchy." Forbidden practices may include fantasizing about men, enjoying penetration with dildos or fingers, and engaging in S/M. However, not all PC lesbians bring their politics to bed with them.

It is fine and wonderful to be politically correct in bed. It is fine and wonderful to be politically incorrect in bed. But the coupling of a PC lesbian and a PI lesbian possesses as much potential for smooth sailing as Phyllis Schlafly and k.d. lang. If you find yourself turned on by someone committed to the other side of the sexual-political border, remember that neither of you owns the moral high ground. You're just different. If you cannot keep your hands off one another, maybe, conceivably, with a great deal of patience, you will discover sex acts for which your belief systems overlap. I'm sure if Phyllis and k.d. really craved each other, they'd find some way to get it on.

Otherwise, you can always skip the sex and go out for coffee.

PORNOGRAPHY. Pornography is a lesbian minefield. Some lesbians believe that all porn promotes violence against women, so they support Women Against Pornography and laws that limit First Amendment rights. These lesbians have even picketed *lesbian* writers, including Susie Bright and Joan Nestle, claiming that their work, too, oppresses women.

Other lesbians distinguish between pornography and erotica, defining *erotica* as more artistic and emotional work featuring non-oppressive and nonviolent depictions of sexuality.

And still other lesbians unabashedly love their porn — although, as Gail says, "I can't talk to all my feminist friends about the fact that I rent these movies. Some would point a finger and say, 'What are you checking out that trash for?'"

This is not to say that pro-porn women watch and support *all* porn; few lesbians consider watching violence against women to be a recreational activity. But many do enjoy watching movies that other lesbians would reject as politically incorrect.

Perhaps the most frequent response to porn is a sort of abashed ambivalence, as Suzanne explains: "The movies are so silly. The women don't look like real women. The acting is bad. My theater sensibilities are offended. But they turn me on."

Since one woman's pornography is another woman's erotica, they are discussed together here; please draw the line where you feel comfortable, and remember: what you like is your business.

Pornography and erotica, like fantasies, are places where sexual boundaries can be ignored. Gail and Alice enjoy Jeff Stryker movies. Kathy and Lydia read gay male porn. Gail also recommends Nina Hartley movies, saying, "She's a feminist, she's bisexual. She's just a delight to watch, whether she's with men or with women. And she's got a great behind."

Gail adds that it helps to have a nice place to rent movies. "I don't have to worry about some guy in a trenchcoat. I go in there like I own the place." (If you don't have access to a safe and comfortable place to buy or rent pornographic movies or books, see *Mail Order.*)

Many women have expressed disappointment with lesbian sex movies, which mostly fall into two categories. The "supposedly-lesbian-but-made-for-men" movies just don't ring true to many women, particularly when the actresses sport inch-long razor-sharp nails. Current lesbian-made sex movies are often cheaply made and unexciting; however, since more lesbians are gaining film experience, the future should bring exciting and polished lesbian-made movies for every taste. *Suburban Dykes* is one example of satisfying lesbian porn.

As camcorders have come down in price, making your own sex movies has become an option. Write a script and get friends to act, or simply point the camera at the bed and press the "on" button. Film yourself making love with your lover — or with yourself — or with a bunch of women. Who knows what ideas you might come up with? (If you lend your camera to someone else, *remember to take out your sex tape* — unless, of course, you want to drop her a huge hint.)

Lesbian-written sex books and magazines are a booming industry. Magazines include *On Our Backs* and *Bad Attitude*, both of which lean toward the hard-core. Books range from Katherine Forrest's totally vanilla and very sexy classic *Curious Wine* to Pat Califia's hard-core *Macho Sluts*, with the anthologies *Bushfire* (edited by Karen Barber) and *Serious Pleasure* (edited by the Sheba Collective) in between. And if nothing turns you on, have patience; more lesbian sex writing is being published all the time.

Another option is to write your own erotica, whether for yourself, for your partner, or for publication. The audience for lesbian sex fiction of all sorts is large and hungry.

If you're new to lesbian sex, erotica and pornography can be educational as well as exciting. But don't expect life to be like porn; real humans are limited by mundane considerations such as exhaustion and muscle cramps. (See also *Books* and the *Resource List*.)

POSITIONS. There are infinite possible positions for lesbian sex; the sky (and your bodies) is the limit.

One fancy position much enjoyed by many lesbians goes by the vivid nickname of "sit on my face." One woman lies on her back, while the other crouches above her with her knees on either side of the first woman's head or shoulders. The woman on top then lowers her vulva (or anus) to the first woman's mouth. This position takes some arranging of arms and legs, and being on top is not for the weak-kneed. On the other hand, being on the bottom is ideal for women with various disabilities, as the entire body can be rested while the tongue and mouth do the work. But make sure your head is strongly supported!

Jenn once suffered broken ribs and cannot lie on her stomach for long periods, so when she goes down on her girlfriend, the girlfriend either lies down on a table or sits with her legs spread over the arms of an armchair.

Oral sex can also be accomplished with one woman standing and the other kneeling or sitting on the floor in front on her. Some women find this position degrading, while others find it very hot. Some find it both!

Tribadism — rubbing together face-to-face — can be nicely done standing. Many lesbians have had orgasms from vertical tribadism — also known as dancing — in women's bars.

For penetration, a very popular position is known as "doggie style." The woman being penetrated gets on her knees, and her partner enters from behind with her fingers or a dildo. Some women prefer to kneel on the floor with their upper body on the bed, while others prefer to be up on their hands and knees. In this position, the woman being penetrated can touch her own clit.

Fancy positions can occur spontaneously in sex, or the partners may decide beforehand they want to try something new. It's amazing how the same old "lick, lick, lick" can feel completely different in a chair rather than in bed or how penetration from behind, rather than in front, can make a sex session sizzle.

Note: When you and your lover find some wonderful and acrobatic position, and you're both sweating and moaning, the last thing you want to do is stop and get a pillow or ask her to move her leg. But do it. The passion won't suddenly evaporate. Why have a stiff neck or back for a day or two if you don't have to?

PRIVACY. If there were a Bill of Rights for sex, the Right to Privacy would be part of it. Whether during a one-night stand or a long-term relationship, people need space in their heads and in their lives. Granting each other this privacy can be as simple as not glancing through her notebook when she goes to the bathroom or as difficult as allowing her to enjoy her friendship with an ex-lover without demanding to know their every move together.

Privacy is a particular challenge in long-term relationships, where two women may get into the habit of discussing their every thought. But some thoughts needn't be shared, including passing sexual attractions to other women and the fact that you hate her haircut. Yes, it is important to discuss differences and clear the air, but it is also nice to give each other a break once in a while. If she's studying for finals, you don't have to let her know that you're pissed at someone at work. Talk to a friend. And each partner doesn't have to know exactly who the other is talking to on the phone.

Allowing a partner privacy can be frightening, particularly if you are unsure of yourself. Why is she pissed?, you may wonder. Who is she talking to? How can we keep our relationship honest if we keep secrets? The answer is to find a balance between privacy and sharing.

A particularly important aspect of privacy occurs around sexual fantasies. Although sharing such fantasies can be exciting, this sharing becomes problematic if, for instance, a woman in a vanilla sex couple fantasies only about hard-core S/M, or one partner often fantasizes about men. But the other partner need not ever know about these fantasies.

Should two women choose to discuss their fantasies, one partner has no right to tell the other to change them. (Though, of course, she has the right to her feelings about them.) No one is entitled to control another person's mind.

Note that seeking privacy does not justify straight-out lying.

There are difficult things to discuss that must be talked about anyway. Privacy does not include the right not to tell your sexual partner you are having a herpes outbreak. Nor does it justify having secret affairs when you are in a monogamous relationship.

As in so many areas of life, it's important to seek a balance.

Q–R

QUICKIES. You're due at your friends' house in thirty minutes, so you and your lover are getting ready to leave. But you become transfixed by the line of her neck as she leans over to tie her shoe. Or you are mesmerized by the way her mouth moves as she puts on her mascara. Or you are turned on by the way her breasts lift as she brushes her hair. You go over and kiss her, and the next thing you know, you're making love on the floor, half-dressed. Welcome to the quickie.

Quickies don't only pop up when you're in a rush. There's the "I-have-to-study, would-you-help-me-relax" quickie. And the "I'd-sure-like-an-orgasm-before-I-go-to-sleep" quickie. And the "Forget-foreplay, I-just-can't-wait" quickie.

Amusingly enough, lesbian quickies aren't always that quick. Gail's quickies last fifteen minutes to half an hour, while Jenn takes an hour or so! Rebecca does occasionally enjoy the intense five or ten minutes of sex without foreplay, but Jessica says, "To me, a quickie's having to take somebody home afterward and not having them spend the night."

Considering that the average heterosexual sexual experience is said to take about ten minutes, and that most lesbian *quickies* last longer, no wonder so many lesbians adore our sexual orientation!

RAPE. See *Consent; Survivors.*

REBOUND RELATIONSHIPS. In the lesbian community, women frequently go from one relationship to the next without stopping to mourn. This is a dangerous habit, since unfelt and unexpressed feelings can poison the new relationship and future ones as well.

Nevertheless, the attraction of a new relationship is clear; the pain of the breakup can be submerged in the excitement of new love. The final months of the old relationship were probably dreadful, with unsatisfying sex — if any. It's easy to think, "Well, that's over. Isn't this new woman cute and smart and sexy and everything my last lover wasn't?" It's easy to jump right in. But old business jumps right in with you.

Not all rebound relationships are destined to fail, but they have much going against them: leftover mourning and resentments, plus expectations that may have more to do with the ex than with the current lover.

If you possibly can, take time to mourn and heal. And remember, you didn't fail; perhaps two years (or six years or six months) was the perfect length for that particular relationship. Before moving forward, leave the past behind. Then, when you do find your next lover, you can love her for herself rather than for the ways in which she differs from your ex. (See also *Ex-Lovers.*)

REJECTION. Everyone gets rejected now and again. But it still hurts. The challenge is to survive the rejection, heal, and perhaps even learn from the experience. For example, if you're into casual sex, and you get some yeses and some nos to your propositions, then rejection is no big deal. Not everyone finds everyone else attractive; not everyone is into casual sex. But if you are *constantly* turned down, it's time to look at yourself. Is your come-on too strong? Are you approaching the wrong people? Do you need a new attitude? A new mouthwash?

Some rejections hurt more than others; having a longtime lover leave is probably the worst. If this happens, you will feel like you got hit by a car, and you may be tempted to drown your sorrow in alcohol or in a new relationship. The best thing you can do for yourself, however, is just go ahead and feel terrible. Mourn. Rant and rave. Bitch endlessly to friends (but do remember to ask them how *they* are — and to listen to the answers — if you want the friendships to survive). Go to a therapist or a support group. Write your ex nasty letters (which you don't have to mail). And stay away from people who don't acknowledge your grief; if your mother says "I'm sorry you lost your roommate" and changes the subject, turn to someone else for comfort.

Because lesbians can't legally marry, lesbian breakups can seem less important than heterosexual divorces, but that's baloney. Splitting up is one of the saddest experiences on earth — for all humans.

In addition, your pain doesn't count less if the breakup was mutual or even if you left her. (One woman complained, "No one writes sad songs for the one who leaves.") No matter which partner says it's over, the ending of a relationship is heartbreaking.

Write from the Heart: Lesbians Healing from Heartache, edited by Anita L. Pace, discusses how some lesbians have survived breakups.

ROMANCE. When it comes to romance, embrace the clichés. What could be more romantic than flowers, dinner at a fancy restaurant, smooching by a roaring fireplace, reading poetry, holding hands at the beach, leaving love notes in surprising places, candlelight, breakfast in bed, and stolen kisses in elevators?

Or base your romantic gestures on her particular fancies. Perhaps she'd like to make love in a bed strewn with rose petals. Maybe she'd like nothing better than sex with you wearing leather chaps. Romance is in the eye of the beholder.

Never ignore the simple romantic gesture. Imagine her delight when your hardworking partner comes home after a long day and you're lying nude on a bed with fresh sheets, a couple of sandwiches, and a big grin.

Romance happens at the place where caring and imagination meet. And if you're short on imagination, caring and clichés will do. (See also *Aphrodisiacs; Long-Term Relationships.*)

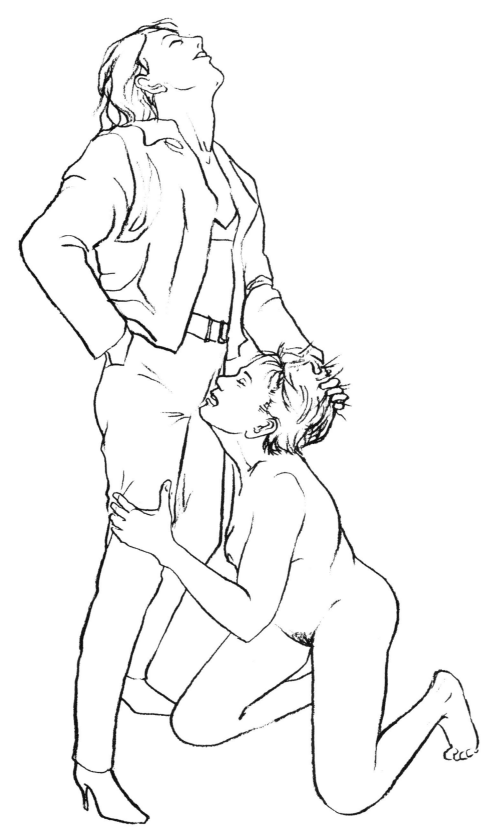

S

SADOMASOCHISM. Much controversy in the lesbian community focuses on S/M. Feel free to ignore the arguments. If you don't want to do S/M, there's no reason you should; if you do want to, there's no reason you shouldn't. You needn't apologize to anyone, whatever type of consensual sex you prefer.

Your level of success seeking an S/M partner will probably depend on where you live. Many metropolitan areas have S/M groups that provide information, safety demonstrations, and opportunities to socialize. Check out the organizational listings in your local lesbian and gay paper; read the personal ads as well. If your locale lacks a gay paper, try the personals in *On Our Backs*. If these approaches don't work, consider starting your own group or publishing your own personal ad.

If you're comfortable doing so, let your friends know of your S/M interest. You may be astonished at their curiosity and experience; in addition, they may know people into S/M or want to play with you themselves. On the other hand, you might get an earful of anti-S/M invective and risk losing some buddies.

When you do meet someone to play with, *be careful*. The world contains some seriously crazy people. S/M requires trustworthiness as well as trust, plus good boundaries, detailed negotiation, and competence.

If you have a partner and you both want to experiment, start slowly. How honest do you dare be with each other? It's one thing to acknowledge that being tied up is attractive, but still another to reveal that nipple clamps turn you on. Even if you've established trust and communication in your relationship, honest conversations about sexual desires can be risky and therefore scary — but they can also be incredibly hot and exciting. Keep each other posted on how you feel, and avoid exclamations like, "Oh, that's disgusting!" A more helpful response might be, "Well, that's not something I want to try just now."

Jessica says, "A lot of times people say that so-called vanilla sex is a 'kinder, gentler' fuck — they wouldn't say 'fuck' though, they'd say 'lovemaking' — but one thing I have learned with S/M is to be really, really open and honest about what you want. To me, S/M, if you really communicate, if you really listen, if you really follow all the guidelines, it's a hell of a lot safer than plain old 'let's-just-go-to-bed-and-have-sex.' S/M almost forces you to sit down and talk about it. I think everybody should do that, regardless of what kind of sex they have."

Alice and her lover occasionally practice S/M, and she says, "We were together over nine months before we even knew each other was interested. It took another year to discover *how* interested." They went from light bondage to full bondage with whipping.

Before having S/M sex, establish a safeword, that is, a word that means "stop." Since one or both of you may want to say "No, no, stop" — without intending that the other will actually stop — the safeword should be unrelated to what you're doing. "Red" for "stop" and "pink" for "easier or less" are traditional choices.

S/M may involve a scenario or "scene." This can be anything you want it to be. Perhaps one of you plays a teacher and the other a pupil; perhaps one of you plays a cop and the other a driver pulled over for speeding; perhaps one of you plays a sergeant and the other a brand-new enlistee. You can set general guidelines before starting, or you can virtually write a play.

For many people, the thrill of S/M is the adrenaline rush. As the combined emotional-physical stimulation heightens, so does the high. However, with pain feeling like pleasure, it's easy to get hurt. Neither partner should be under the influence of drugs or alcohol; limits set before you start must be honored throughout the scene.

If you want to limit your S/M to a little experimentation, bondage and blindfolds are popular toys to start with. The occasional slap on the butt can be added. For many women, this is kinky enough.

But for others, S/M offers its own world of experiences and sensations. Jessica explains, "I have a chronic illness, and I used to be very athletic. I loved the physical high that I got off cycling. It was absolutely wonderful. Now it's often hard for me to get out of my physical space. Sex is one of the ways I can get beyond feeling lousy and S/M intensifies that. If I'm being whipped or something, it reminds me a lot of cycling, just being totally high off all those endorphins. It's like I move beyond this dimension of reality."

From gentle scenes to hard-core pain, from foreplay to lifestyle, a book could be written about S/M. And it has been; *Coming to Power* mixes philosophy, advice, erotic fiction, and photographs for a complete introduction to S/M. Also check out Pat Califia's *Lesbian S/M Safety Manual*.

SAFER SEX. What follows is a somewhat unorthodox safer-sex discussion, as it does not focus on AIDS. Female-to-female HIV transmission is believed by many scientists to be highly inefficient (see *AIDS*); however, herpes, crabs, scabies, yeast infections, venereal warts, trichomoniasis, and even hepatitis are easily spread from woman to woman (see *Sexually Transmitted Diseases*). Therefore, this discussion centers on general sexual hygiene and safety guidelines. You can adjust these guidelines to suit your own needs and comfort with taking risks.

Some women believe that precautions are unnecessary when having sex with women because "lesbians don't get STDs." But we do — from men and from each other. Most lesbians have had sex with men; many still do. In addition, past experience with intravenous drug use is not rare in the lesbian community. And remember: *people sometimes lie about their pasts.*

General guidelines: For absolute 1,000 percent safety from any sexually transmitted diseases, stick to celibacy or long-term monogamy with an uninfected lover. However, even a totally faithful partner can come down with a yeast or bladder infection; to avoid catching it, do not go down on your partner until she is cured, and wash your hands thoroughly after touching her genitals. In addition, unprotected anilingus *always* carries some health risk.

When having sex with multiple partners, particularly those whose histories you do not know, there is always some risk of catching an STD. Even sharing towels or clothing or using someone else's toilet (or a public toilet for that matter) carries a small risk of getting crabs and scabies.

The following breakdown of safe, possibly safe, and unsafe practices is based on HIV transmission guidelines but is also useful for avoiding other STDs.

Safe. Practices considered generally safe for lesbian sex include massages, hugging, closed-mouth kissing (unless a cold sore is present), tribadism, masturbating together (with each touching her own genitals), S/M without exchanging body fluids or coming into contact with fecal matter, reading erotica together, and watching each other masturbate.

Possibly safe. Practices considered possibly safe include protected cunnilingus and anilingus (that is, through a piece of latex, such as a dental dam or cut-open condom), finger-to-genital contact or vaginal or anal penetration using a disposable latex glove or finger cots, and open-mouthed kissing (also known as tongue kissing, wet kissing, or French kissing).

Unsafe. Practices considered unsafe include unprotected cunnilingus and anilingus, directly touching the vagina or anus (particularly if you have a cut on your hand or fingers), and sharing sex toys that have had contact with the partner's body fluids. In addition, having unprotected vaginal or anal intercourse with a man and sharing needles are always unsafe.

Keep in mind: If you choose not to practice safer sex as a rule, you may still want to adjust your behavior under certain circumstances. For instance, if you have an open herpes sore or an oral yeast infection, you may be at higher risk for catching an infection; however, under these circumstances, you should be practicing safer sex for your partner's sake! Another time for caution may be during menstruation; it's probably best to avoid contact with menstrual blood orally and, if you have cuts on your hands, manually. In addition, if you believe that HIV is transmissible orally via gum disease, don't practice cunnilingus without a dental dam *whether or not your partner has her period.* Gum disease is so prevalent that it's safest to assume that you *do* have it.

Dental dams. Dental dams are pieces of latex through which cunnilingus or anilingus can be performed. They are available at medical supply stores, condom stores, and some women's health services. If you can't find dental dams in your area, buy condoms and cut them open.

Using dental dams takes some practice, as they can be difficult to hold. Always keep track of which side of the dental dam has touched the anus or vulva. In addition, vaginal secretions can sometimes overflow the dental dam; if you are seeking total safety, and her lubrication is getting past the dental dam, it's time to stop the proceedings. Washing your partner's pubic area to get rid of overflowing vaginal fluid is disruptive, but it's a practical way to avoid this problem.

If you put a dental dam down and cannot remember which side contacted the vulva or anus, it's time for a new dental dam.

Lydia says, "I think it's horrendous that they have not figured out something that women can use that is bigger than a dental dam and offers more protection. All they need is the same thing, but just longer and wider — like a sheet. That way it could be held tauter, so it doesn't get sucked into your nose or your mouth."

She continues, "A lot of women can't eroticize safer sex, and they don't bother with dental dams. Instead, they're getting more into penetration and they're getting more into other forms of sex, basically because oral sex is so hard — you don't want to take those chances."

In recognition of these problems, Good Vibrations sells an item called "Dammit." As the catalogue describes it, "two adjustable leather thigh straps hold a dam in place over the genital area so your hands are free to seek other pleasures." The Dammit is not cheap ($20), but if it improves your sex life and your safety, it's worth the money.

Gloves. Latex gloves are available through medical supply stores and drugstores. Avoid the powdered kind. Gloves provide protection during penetration; they also cover rough hands and uneven nails with a smooth surface. Don't absentmindedly touch your mouth, eyes, or vagina with your gloved hand once it has touched your partner's vagina or anus.

Condoms. Of course, the lesbian who still has sex with men must insist that they use condoms for safety. But condoms can also keep dildos and vibrators from turning into STD transmitters. Even monogamous couples sometimes use condoms on their sex toys to avoid sharing the occasional yeast infection.

Visiting the doctor. Since so many STDs are asymptomatic in women, sexually adventurous lesbians should consider having regular STD evaluations, perhaps yearly when they have their Pap smears.

The happy ending. Lydia has discovered that adjusting to safer sex practices can actually enhance sex; she explains that, "Putting condoms on dildos or putting on latex gloves has gotten to be kind of fun in a rather kinky way. It's a trigger now that sex is going to happen."

SAFETY.

Vibrators. Some women like to keep their vibrator plugged in next to the bed, ready for use. However, if you have animals you might want to try another approach. One woman, after a lovely night of sex, rushed off to work in the morning. Somehow, her vibrator had ended up under a pillow, still plugged in. And, somehow, one of the cats turned it on. When the woman got home from work, she found a shorted-out vibrator and a burned pillow. Only great luck kept her house from burning down.

Vibrators are electric appliances that must be treated with respect.

Alcohol and drug use. Being drunk or stoned lessens inhibitions, raises pain tolerance, and impairs judgment, so avoid any sort of S/M when you or your partner is under the influence. Safer sex is also better performed sober.

Penetration. When using vegetables or household items for penetration, take time to examine what you're using. Vegetables often have little hairs or rough parts. Bottles can break. Avoid open bottles since thrusting them in and out can create suction on your insides; there is a story, perhaps an urban legend, about a woman who bled to death after jerking a suctioned bottle out of her vagina. Be careful! If something does get stuck in your vagina through this vacuum effect, simply use your fingers to open your vagina wider and break the seal.

Hyperpenetration. Women occasionally get items stuck in their vaginas or anuses. Unless you feel that you have pierced yourself internally — in which case go immediately to an emergency room or call 911! — the best thing you can do is *relax.* After you have calmed down considerably, squat and push with your pelvic muscles, as though you are having a bowel movement. Whatever was stuck may come out pretty easily. If not, relax for a while and try again. Don't be shy about reaching inside yourself and pulling the item out.

If you simply can't get the lost item out, consider asking a friend for help, or make that visit to the doctor.

SCENTS. Getting ready for a big night? First time to the women's bar? First date? Think twice before you splash on that cologne. Many lesbians suffer from chemical sensitivities, and the same amount of perfume that might be fine in most of the world may be considered too much in a lesbian setting. (Nonlesbians suffer from chemical sensitivities as well, but lesbians have been one of the first groups to take the subject seriously.) It's a highly personal topic; one women's gentle scent is another women's headache. But, just as nonsmokers no longer accept breathing in other people's smoke, chemically sensitive women are growing less willing to breathe in other people's perfume.

SEDUCTION. *To seduce* means "to convince someone to have sex," but it also means "to win over, to entice." In pragmatic terms, seduction need not take long. But it can also be savored, extended, and enjoyed, for minutes, days, even years.

A key to seduction is that "firsts" only happen once, including the first time having sex. Use that limitation to advantage by meting out the firsts slowly. First date, first hand holding, first hug, first kiss, and first sex can all happen in one night, but there's joy in making them last longer. Done artfully, presexual play sizzles — and the lovemaking that follows may be more sexy, intense, and tender when it does happen.

Take time to flirt. Leave sweet messages on each other's phone machines. Bring flowers and candy. Spend entire evenings making out. Give each other massages. Hold hands while watching romantic movies. Look into each other's eyes. *Relish every second.* The slower the seduction goes, the longer it lasts!

SEX. Here's an entire book about sex, but what *is* sex?

The dictionary talks about biology and genders and then offers "sexual intercourse." Turn to *intercourse* and you find "conversation" and "coitus." *Coitus* is defined as "sexual intercourse." Not much help.

Then there are the popular definitions. In Kathy's high school, the rule was that sex occurred only when a male put his penis in a female's vagina. This allowed teenage girls who had practiced cunnilingus, fellatio, and humping to orgasm to assure their mothers they were still virgins. By this definition, lesbians never have sex!

Another popular definition claims that sex is activity ending in orgasm. But what about women who are nonorgasmic? Have they

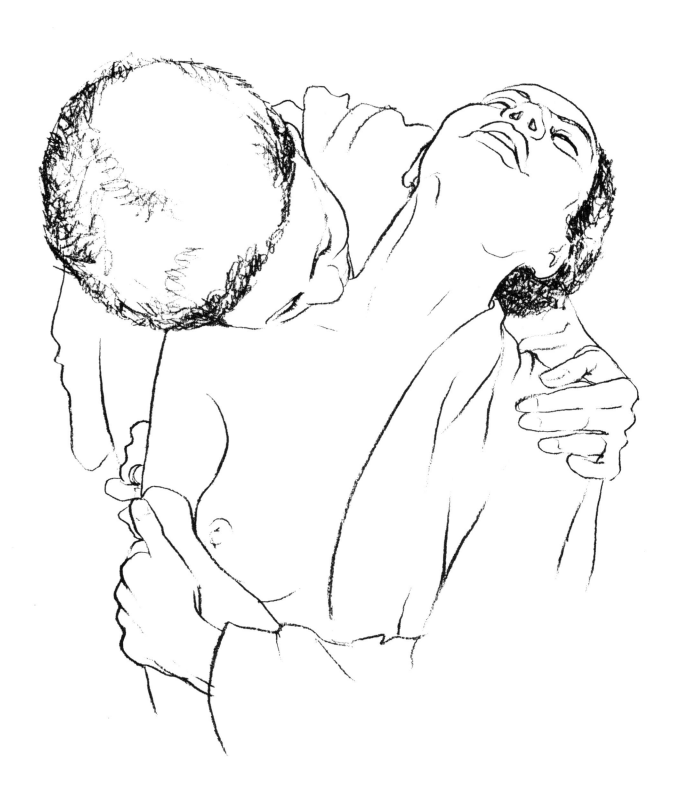

never had sex? If two women make love and only one comes, did the other not have sex?

Mainstream definitions of sex obviously ignore lesbians, but we can ignore them right back! Each and every lesbian can define sex personally, with or without penetration, with or without foreplay, with or without love, with or without cunnilingus, with or without orgasms.

SEX AND LOVE ADDICTION. How much sex is too much sex? For many women, that's a downright silly question. But for others, the desire for sex — and for love — may grow into obsession, with more and more anxiety and less and less pleasure as time goes on. There's no absolute measure of when a healthy and enthusiastic libido steps over the line into addiction, and if you enjoy the amount of sex you are having, that's all that counts. But if you don't, if you find yourself unable to say "no" even when you want to, if you lose time at work to get laid or masturbate, and if you compulsively pursue sex, then you might want to check out the 12-step program of Sexaholics Anonymous (SA), based on Alcoholics Anonymous.

On the other hand, you may not.

The problem with SA (as well as Sex Addicts Anonymous, Sexual Compulsives Anonymous, and Sex and Love Addicts Anonymous) is that it's altogether too willing to label as obsessive behavior that is within the realm of normal variation. For instance, one SA pamphlet asks, "Although your spouse is sexually compatible, do you still masturbate or have sex with others?" But why is masturbation a problem in a relationship? The same pamphlet asks, "Do you feel guilt, remorse, or depression after sex?" If you do, it may be a sign of sex addiction, but it may also be a sign of childhood sexual abuse or growing up in a hyper-religious home. Another pamphlet says, "Emotional consequences [of compulsive sexual addiction include] guilt about behaviors that are against one's values, such as affairs, *same gender sex*, abortions, lying, or suicidal thoughts" [italics mine].

If you are worried, consider the root of your sexual behavior. Perhaps you suffer from low self-esteem because of childhood sexual abuse. Or perhaps you are so glad to be out of the closet that all you want to do is party your ass off. Maybe you need therapy — or maybe you should just go ahead and party for a while. But if your situation seems chronic and insoluble, then think about seeking help at SA.

If you do, be careful to find a meeting that includes other lesbians and gay men or that is clearly pro-gay. Otherwise, you may find your sexual orientation rather than your compulsive behavior being treated as the problem. In addition, beware of anyone who suggests that you go to Homosexuals Anonymous; HA treats your lesbianism as an addiction/disease and supposedly helps you to become heterosexual!

To find a meeting, look in your phone book under Sexaholics Anonymous, Sex and Love Addicts Anonymous, Sex Addicts Anonymous, and Sexual Compulsives Anonymous.

SEX CLUBS. (Bars, clubs, or bathhouses where lesbians can have anonymous sex on the premises.)

Periodically, lesbian sex clubs open — and close. Sometimes one springs up in the back room of a lesbian bar; other times, a straight or gay men's establishment will set one night aside for women. Usually based in large cities, the lesbian sex clubs tend to fold due to lack of clientele; traditionally, too few gay women enjoy anonymous sex to keep a business open. However, with a new generation of lesbians pushing the sexual boundaries, these sex clubs may have finally come into their own.

As of this writing, sex clubs exist at least one evening a week in Los Angeles, San Francisco, and New York. Depending on the clientele, the sex that occurs may be vanilla or S/M, two-by-two or in groups. The word "no" is strongly respected, although Donna Minkowitz writes in the *Village Voice*, "In the seconds it takes to get used to the dark, I'm having my nipples stroked from behind by a woman I don't know. *This is everything I ever wanted.*" In other words, if you want to say "no," you had best say it quickly, and if you want to say "no" often, perhaps sex clubs are just not for you.

If you do try sex clubs, decide beforehand what your safer-sex limitations and needs are; if you feel a need for latex or gloves, bring your own. Also keep in mind that such clubs are occasionally raided by the police. In addition, watch out for men sneaking in, as occurred at one of the clubs Minkowitz wrote about.

SEXUAL GROWTH. Women whose sexuality does not include every possible sort of orgasm and response are often called "dysfunctional." The dictionary definition of *dysfunction* refers to "disorder" and "impairment." When talking about kidneys or lungs, a disorder can be objectively judged, but sexual impairments are in the eyes of the beholder. If a woman rarely has orgasms or doesn't enjoy penetration, she is "impaired" only if she *wants* more orgasms or would *like* to enjoy being penetrated. "Sexual growth" was chosen as the name of this entry because it is more positive than "sexual dysfunction," and it acknowledges that sexuality is fluid, with endless potential. A great deal of specific information on how to expand your sexual responses can be found in this book and many others; however, the most important thing to keep in mind is this: *Growth is always possible* — no matter what a woman's age or background or physical or psychological situation.

Kathy describes the steady growth she has experienced in her orgasmic response since her late teens: "When I first started masturbating, I didn't have an orgasm for over a year. Then I started having little ones, then bigger ones. It took me a long time to come, sometimes over an hour, but I'd get there. When I first started having sex with other people, I wasn't able to come from being licked or touched by someone else. I was too nervous, and I just couldn't ask anyone to stimulate me for as long as I needed. Then I met a woman with incredible stamina, who told me she could and would lick me all day if I wanted. Just knowing she wouldn't stop and that she enjoyed licking me gave me the freedom to come, though it did take a long time. After a while, though, it didn't take quite as long. As time passed, I was able to come quicker and quicker. Now I find that sometimes I actually try to delay my orgasm."

Orgasms. Dr. Emily L. Sisley and Bertha Harris wrote in *The Joy of Lesbian Sex* that, "unless they are temporarily incapacitated — stoned, ill, quite preoccupied or the like — lesbians *always* reach orgasm in their lovemaking." Sisley and Harris were wrong, and their blatant *"always"* left many nonorgasmic and preorgasmic women wondering if they were indeed lesbians.

If you have trouble having orgasms, you are not alone. *The Gay Report,* a 1977 book discussing the responses of 962 lesbians (and 4,329 gay men) to a questionnaire about their sex lives, reported that 10 percent to 20 percent of the lesbians surveyed had orgasms infrequently or not at all. The same book also reported that 91 percent of lesbian respondents considered having an orgasm very important or somewhat important and 94 percent considered their partner having an orgasm very important or somewhat important. Of the respondents to JoAnn Loulan's survey in the more recent *Lesbian Passion,* 12 percent were dissatisfied with their sex lives because of "orgasmic problems."

Obviously, lesbian sex is not the simple experience Sisley and Harris would have us believe, and lesbians are not superhuman lovers — nor should we be. Growing up as women in a sexist, antisex society, we are as prone as straight women to sexual limitations.

Since cunnilingus is more efficient than penile intercourse at causing orgasms in women, some people assume that lesbians get over their preorgasmic stage quicker than straight women. But that assumption is not always true; some lesbians don't even practice oral sex. However, many women who did not have orgasms with male lovers do have them with female lovers.

If you are nonorgasmic or barely orgasmic, consider where you are now and what you want to accomplish. Are orgasms important to you? To your partner? Can you come from masturbation? Using a vibrator? Would you be able to come if you weren't worrying about your lover's jaw growing tired or tongue giving out? Do you want to come *just* to please your partner?

If you've never had an orgasm, and want to, make time to masturbate regularly. Take the phone off the hook, light a candle, and put on nice music. Fantasize. Add erotic movies or books, if you're comfortable with them.

Being physically fit can help you come, so practice your Kegel exercises. Also, early orgasms can take a lot of work, so try using a vibrator. Vibrators are steady and strong, they never get tired or cranky, and they never give up.

Whatever approach you take, don't expect results immediately. Focus on your pleasurable sensations moment by moment rather than worrying about future orgasms. Most importantly, have fun and be nice to yourself. Achieving an orgasm is a present to yourself, not a test you must pass to be a complete woman.

If you can make yourself come but cannot achieve orgasm with your lover, one of the first obstacles to deal with will be her ego. Her feelings may be hurt, particularly if she believes that you don't come because she's a bad lover or you don't really care about her. Talk to each other honestly and openly about your needs. Reassure her that your lack of orgasm is not about her, and ask for her help — and her patience. Be honest about what you need to come, be it steady stimulation, time, quiet, or even privacy. Sometimes, just her assurance that she wants you and enjoys sex whether or not you come will make coming easier.

Ask your partner to take the responsibility to let you know if she gets tired, so that you can lie back and enjoy what she does without worrying about her. If you take a long time, or if you prefer to make yourself come, perhaps she can go down on you for a while, then pleasure you elsewhere while you touch yourself or use a vibrator.

For both of you, making love will improve a great deal if orgasm is treated as one part of sex rather than the be-all and end-all of life itself.

If your partner does not meet your needs or persists in seeing your lack of orgasms as a personal attack, you will be unlikely ever to come with her. A different partner might be helpful. The best lover is the one who accepts and enjoys you as you are rather than as she thinks you should be.

For more exercises and ideas to help you achieve the orgasmic fulfillment you desire, see JoAnn Loulan's *Lesbian Sex* and *For Yourself* by Lonnie Garfield Barbach. The assistance and guidance of a qualified therapist might also be helpful.

Penetration. For some women, penetration remains an occasional extra rather than a mainstay of their sex lives, and they are totally comfortable with that. For others, sex isn't sex without penetration. Still others don't enjoy penetration or object to it for political reasons.

If you want to enjoy penetration more than you do, the primary requirement is complete trust in your partner, which will take time. Explain in advance that penetration is scary or unpleasant for you. Ask that she not go inside unless you invite her in — and that she then do only what you ask her to. While this may seem pushy or demanding, you are simply setting the boundaries you need to enjoy yourself. If your partner handles your request badly, she's not the best partner for you at this time.

When practicing with yourself or a highly trusted lover, start with one finger inside you, not moving, and see how that feels. Add movement or more fingers if you want to; however, that one steady finger may be all you ever desire.

If your discomfort with penetration results from past abuse in your life, therapy may be necessary before you can totally reclaim your sexuality.

Your response to penetration, whatever it is, reaches "functional" when *you* are happy with it.

General. If you have been abused sexually in the past, you may have an erratic sex drive, only occasionally feeling comfortable with sex. Or particular parts of your body may need protecting. As Suzanne explains, "The neck is a problematic area for me. It's really erogenous, but if I'm at all panicky — do not touch, back off."

Some women feel detached from their feelings or cannot concentrate on sex. If you are one, you may ultimately choose to see a therapist; however, there are many things you can do to start reclaiming your feelings on your own. A good first step is to allow yourself to say no when you need to and to be kind to yourself when you do so. This kindness includes avoiding partners who criticize your sexual response.

Keeping a journal can help you ascertain the roots of your body discomforts. As you grow to understand yourself better, listen to your needs and try to meet them. You are the best judge of what might help you. You may decide to remain celibate for a while. You may try dating. Or something as simple as positive self-talk may make all the difference. As only one example, Kathy, an incest survivor, sometimes repeats her lover's name over and over in her head as a sort of mantra to remind herself that she is with someone she trusts and loves and who will not hurt her.

Most importantly, always remember that not being able to relax and enjoy sex does not mean that you are bad and something's wrong with you; it means that there are ways you want to grow. (See also *Communication; G-Spot; Kegel Exercises; Survivors; Therapists; Vaginal Orgasms;* and the *Resource List.)*

SEXUALLY TRANSMITTED DISEASES. Legend has it that "the only people to get fewer STDs than lesbians are nuns," but that legend relies heavily on stereotypes about both lesbians *and* nuns. While STDs are less prevalent in the lesbian community than in many others, they occur sufficiently often to be of concern to the sexually active woman.

Some of the following STDs are more easily transmitted through lesbian sex than others. However, since lesbians are constantly re-defining the limits of female-to-female sex, and since some self-defined lesbians still have sex with men, all are appropriate to include here.

Many of these diseases cause few if any distinct symptoms in women, so sexually active nonmonogamous lesbians (particularly those who have sex with men) should consider asking their doctors to regularly monitor them for all STDs — perhaps yearly, when they have their Pap smears. Also, since knowledge is constantly growing about these diseases, it is important to keep up with the latest discoveries and breakthroughs. *Ms.* magazine is a good source of information on women's health issues.

In this discussion, the treatments recommended lean toward traditional Western medicine. For alternate treatment ideas, see *The New Our Bodies, Ourselves; Sapphistry;* and *Alive and Well.*

Catching an STD does not make you a bad person, just as catching the flu does not make you a bad person. However, you must inform your sexual partners that you have an STD before you start sex so that you can use the appropriate safer sex practices. If you discover a new STD, inform all recent partners so that they can seek diagnosis and treatment. In addition, if you find you have crabs, lice, or scabies, inform your housemates and recent visitors as well.

AMEBIASIS. Usually transmitted though anilingus, this disease may result from any sexual practice in which ameba-infected fecal matter comes in contact with a partner's mouth. Since some people have amebiasis asymptomatically, it is possible to get it from a partner who is not ill. Symptoms include bloody diarrhea and abdominal cramps. Amebiasis is difficult to diagnose and to treat; no drug is always 100 percent successful. *Giardiasis,* most frequently found in gay men, is a similar disease. *Shigellosis,* a bacterial infection, is also spread by anal-oral contact; it may produce no symptoms or sudden fever, cramps, and diarrhea. Unlike amebiasis and giardiasis, shigellosis can go away on its own with time; however, drink plenty of fluids while the diarrhea continues, and take antidiarrheal medicine only under a doctor's supervision.

CHLAMYDIA. Chlamydia trachomatis often causes no symptoms until it has spread through the fallopian tubes and caused pelvic inflam-matory disease. Chlamydia is treated with antibiotics. If you have a history of unprotected sex with men, consider being tested for chlamydia just to be safe.

CRABS. Crabs, or crab lice, are considered to be the most easily spread of STDs; they are also transmitted through shared towels or even toilet seats. Roughly a month after infection, these tiny creatures, which can be seen with the naked eye, cause seriously unpleasant itching in the pubic area. Kwell (gamma benzene hexachloride) is the prescription medicine of choice; in addition, combing the pubic hair with a fine-toothed comb can remove the lice eggs. Shaving off your pubic hair may provide some relief. Wash your underwear, clothing, and bedding in hot water; warn your sex partners and housemates to check themselves for crabs or to use Kwell.

Body lice and head lice should also be treated with Kwell. For body lice, Kwell must be slathered over your entire body; for head lice, wash your hair with Kwell shampoo. Body lice are even more transmissible than crabs, so make sure everyone who has used your towels or bedding knows to check for lice or to have a doctor's examination. Head lice are sometimes mistaken for a scalp rash or eczema.

CYSTITIS. Cystitis, also know as urinary tract infection, is not an STD per se, although it can be caused by too-vigorous vaginal penetration or penetration with insufficient lubrication. Cystitis may also result from other irritations to the urethral opening, including chaffing from too-tight or ill-fitting clothing. Cystitis has two main symptoms: urinary frequency (you have to go to the bathroom *all the time)* and a burning feeling during urination. There may also be abdominal and lower back pain.

Sulfa drugs cure cystitis. However, African-American women should not take such drugs until being tested for an inherited deficiency of the blood enzyme G6PD; if you have this not-uncommon deficiency, sulfa drugs can kill you! Women with cystitis can help themselves by drinking plenty of fluids, particularly water and cranberry juice, and avoiding alcohol and caffeine. Vitamin C also helps, as does wearing cotton underwear. For some women, these measures will end the cystitis without the need for medication.

GONORRHEA. Gonorrhea, which can be treated by antibiotics, often remains asymptomatic in women until pelvic inflammatory disease develops; however, there may be vaginal or anal discharge or a general feeling of flu. Although considered rare in the lesbian community, it is not unheard of, and people who have no symptoms are still contagious. If you are sexually active with multiple partners, consider being tested for gonorrhea yearly when you have your Pap smear.

HEPATITIS. While hepatitis A is transmitted through contact with fecal matter, hepatitis B appears in bodily fluids and is transmitted somewhat like HIV. However, hep B transmits more easily than HIV, and infection can result from oral sex or even sharing a toothbrush or drinking glass. In addition, hep A can be caught from unsanitary food or contaminated water or raw shellfish. Symptoms of both include early-stage fever, headache, loss of appetite, joint aches, and rash. Later-stage symptoms include a distinctive yellow color to the eyes and skin known as jaundice plus chalky stools and dark urine. Both hep A and hep B can be treated with bed rest.

People with hepatitis must avoid alcohol and take medication under a doctor's supervision. In addition, they must use separate dishes, towels, bedding, and toilet seats to avoid spreading infection, and they must not prepare other people's food.

HERPES. The virus herpes simplex I usually causes cold sores on the mouth, while herpes simplex II most often results in genital sores. However, oral sex can easily transmit HS I infection to the genitals and HS II infection to the mouth. Herpes is usually contagious only when it is visible during an outbreak, though some people believe it is transmissible a day or two earlier. Between outbreaks, the virus is believed to stay latent, with outbreaks triggered by stress, illness, friction, and the menstrual cycle.

Herpes sores appear as blisters or ulcers, often painful, in the mouth or throat or vagina, although genital herpes sores may take a different appearance; if you have any sort of odd bumps or marks on your genitals, have your doctor check them out. There may be itching and burning in the infected area or flu-like symptoms such as headache, fever, and vomiting. Although there is no cure, the antiviral drug Acyclovir can make outbreaks shorter and less severe.

SCABIES. Microscopic relatives of spiders, scabies can be transmitted by sex or by shared sheets and towels. Itching, which is especially bad at night, starts roughly a month after infection. As with crabs, Kwell is the treatment of choice; however, since scabies females lay their eggs subcutaneously, Kwell must be applied to the entire body and left on for up to a day, with a second treatment ten days later to get the scabies babies. Be sure to get plenty of Kwell underneath your fingernails. In addition, any clothing or bedding that has been in touch with infected skin must be cleaned, and housemates and sex partners must be warned to treat themselves.

Even after the scabies are gone, itching can continue for some time. If the itching is accompanied by red marks or blisters, repeated treatment may be necessary.

SYPHILIS. Another disease with few distinct symptoms in women, untreated syphilis can ultimately be fatal. Caused by a spirochete (a slender, twisted microorganism), first-stage syphilis may cause a painless ulcer (or "chancre") around the opening to the vagina. Secondary-stage symptoms may include rash, swollen lymph nodes, hair loss, and flu — or none of these. Left untreated, syphilis can cause insanity and death.

Most cases of syphilis can be cured by antibiotics. If you are sexually active with multiple partners, get tested for syphilis at least once a year, possibly twice.

TRICHOMONIASIS. Four to twenty-eight days after infection, trich causes a truly icky, green and smelly vaginal discharge. In addition, there can be redness of the genitals, itching, and pain while urinating. Trich may spread easily through sex, shared clothing or towels, and toilet seats; it is treated by the prescription drug Flagyl, which may cause nausea and headaches. Don't drink alcohol while taking Flagyl (or for a few days before or after).

VENEREAL WARTS. Caused by viruses, venereal warts can be transmitted by hand-to-genital and hand-to-anus contact. In addition, once they find a human home, they spread themselves beyond the location where infection first occurred. Although anal warts can itch and bleed after bowel movements or anal intercourse, the warts generally do not hurt. Treatment possibilities include application of the medication Podophyllin, lasers, and surgery. Warts are tenacious, and more than one treatment may be needed; without treatment, warts may eventually become cancerous.

YEAST INFECTIONS. Also known as *candidiasis* or *monilia,* yeast infections are transmissible from woman to woman through sex, shared clothing or towels, and toilet seats; they can also result from too much sugar intake, stress, taking certain medications, and tight clothing. The main symptom is a vaginal discharge resembling cottage cheese, often accompanied by unbearable vaginal itching.

Over-the-counter medications are now available for yeast infections, although first-time sufferers should see a doctor for a definitive diagnosis. If you use an OTC medication, save the applicator in case you want to self-treat future infections.

To self-treat yeast infections, insert two tablespoons of unsweetened and unflavored yogurt into your vagina twice a day using a vaginal applicator. Use a tampon to hold the yogurt in. Vaginal applicators are sold to apply spermicidal foam, or you may have saved one from a medication used to treat an earlier infection.

The yeast that causes infection lives in your body all the time; infection occurs when something throws your body's balance out of whack, such as taking antibiotics. When you do take antibiotics, eat yogurt daily so that the medication does not tip your body's scales in favor of an infection.

In general: If you itch, have redness or swelling, or suffer from any other genital symptoms, forget the myth of the superclean lesbian and go see your doctor. If you are sexually active with many partners, have regular checkups for STDs when you have your yearly Pap smear. (See also *Doctors.*)

SHAVING. Fashions in shaving underarms and legs vary by decade and location in the United States. For many years, particularly the 1950s and early 1960s, shaving was required for a woman to be considered attractive and "natural." With the advent of feminism, letting body hair grow became a badge of pride and identity in certain circles.

Jessica's experience sums up the process some women go through in accepting body hair: "When I first came out, I remember thinking unshaven women looked odd. I thought, Oh, gross. Then my first lover didn't shave, and she was so sexy and attractive. After a while, it just became normal. And now, when I see women who do shave their legs, I think they look like Barbie Dolls. So, I actually prefer body hair."

But Jessica does occasionally shave one place — her head: "I find my shaved head to be very erotic, as do other women." And shaved pubic hair is also fashionable, with some women removing it all and others opting for designs such as heart shapes.

Any given lesbian might shave her underarms but not her legs — or both, but only occasionally — or just her legs, to look acceptable at work — or both, except during vacation. Some extremely butch women shave their underarms and legs, and some seemingly conservative women have hair on their legs but not on their crotches.

One woman shaved her pubic hair to seek relief from a case of the crabs and discovered that, sans pubic hair, she could have orgasms simply by walking in her favorite tight jeans. She continued shaving long after the crabs were gone.

SIMULTANEOUS ORGASMS. Simultaneous orgasms endure more in legend than in practice. As Suzanne says, "It's just too hard to completely let go and be touching or licking her at the same time." Jessica fears getting so lost in her own orgasm that she forgets to continue whatever stimulation is causing her lover's.

Not one of the women interviewed for this book considers simultaneous orgasms important to her sex life; each takes turns making love to her partner and being made love to. The one woman interviewed who had experienced simultaneous Os with any frequency explained that she and her lover are both multiorgasmic and sometimes they just happen to come at the same time. That seems to be the main way simultaneous Os occur: accidentally.

However, achieving simultaneous orgasms is certainly possible for women who care to extend the effort. First, consider the ways in which it is easiest for you and your lover to come. Perhaps you will lick her while she masturbates you. Or you may both touch yourselves so that you can focus your energy on timing rather than technique.

Find a nice comfortable position, as this may take a while. Even a method that usually gets you off instantaneously may be slower when you are dividing your concentration and sexual energy between yourself and your partner. If you both usually come easily, let each other know how close you are to orgasm. Simple words give enough information: "Soon," "Not yet," "Now!" If, however, you are more easily orgasmic than your partner, you'll need to control your timing to match hers — or vice versa.

Whatever method you use, if you manage simultaneous orgasms on your first try, let the *Guinness Book of World Records* know.

SIXTY-NINE. In the 69 position, you and your partner lie next to each other (or one on top of the other), face to vulva and vulva to face, and go down on each other at the same time. But, as with simultaneous orgasms, 69 succeeds more often in fantasy than in real life. What two women have torsos and tongues of exactly the same length? How does the woman underneath breathe? When lying on your sides, where do your legs go? Sixty-nining is a challenge, indeed.

But it's a challenge worth trying, particularly if you do it for closeness and mutuality rather than as a means to achieve orgasms. Sixty-nine is not a position to ease into smoothly and in passionate silence; it takes direction giving and information sharing. Make sure the heavier woman is on the bottom and that her head is sufficiently propped up; 69-ing can all too easily cause a strained neck. Most importantly, make sure both women can breathe!

When 69 works, magic happens. Bodies feel sealed together. Mutual sensations dart back and forth as she does to you what you do to her and your passion grows together. What a wonderful way to spend time.

And if you do both come, congratulations!

SKIN. See *Touch*.

SLEEPING TOGETHER. There are few things in life as cozy, sweet, and downright wonderful as cuddling up against your lover after sex and drifting off to sleep. But this is a joy that may take getting used to. Even after uninhibited sex, sleeping together may bring on floods of self-consciousness and shyness. Worries about snoring, drooling, and how you will look in tomorrow's daylight certainly don't lead to carefree snoozing. And what if she falls asleep on your arm and then you have to move it? These concerns can be intimidating if you want to make a perfect impression.

Forget perfection. You may well snore, and so may she. If you're shy about being nude, put on some clothing; if you're at her place, she'll certainly lend you a t-shirt to sleep in. If you need to turn over in the middle of the night, turn over. You may wake her up with your movement, but that's fine. (It might even lead to more sex!) And yes, you may have bad breath in the morning, but so will she. You're not the only one who's human. This is life, not a movie.

On the other hand, if you just don't care to sleep together, don't. However, if you do want to see her again, be clear about why you are leaving or it will seem that you are rejecting her. (See also *Cuddling; Spoons.*)

SOBER SEX. Drug and alcohol abuse are intimately entwined with some lesbians' sex lives. Chemically dependent women may never have sex clean and sober; the only way they can break all of society's rules and touch a woman is to drink and use. Or they may experience sober sex occasionally, amid the habit of drinking and using.

When chemically dependent women get clean and sober, sex often becomes scary. A newly clean and sober woman may be full of fears: Will I be able to enjoy myself and let go? Will sex be as intense as it was when I used? Will I have the nerve to ask someone out, let alone kiss her or make love with her? What if all the feelings I've drowned for years come flooding in?

Those fears are totally reasonable. Some lesbians do find that their sex lives diminish with sobriety as they become more discerning and sensitive. Women who used to pick up a few partners a week may find that they now prefer to go to bed early, alone. In addition, early sober sex often feels tentative and more inhibited than sex on drugs, and sensations and orgasms may be less intense. And, yes, those old feelings you've been avoiding do come flooding in. Beginning sobriety is a difficult and sensitive time.

But sober sex offers many improvements over stoned sex. As one woman said, "It's better when I remember her name in the morning." And with sobriety comes enhanced sensitivity and consciousness. A woman who once preferred aggressive energetic sex may now desire a quieter, more intense experience; sobriety allows more delicate feelings to come through, including a deep sensuousness and openness. These feelings can be scary, but they are wonderful too.

And as time passes and the chemically dependent woman has more experience being sober, and as she grows through therapy and 12-step programs, her sex life may grow a great deal. Many women experience a sort of renaissance, and their newfound deeper feelings reunite with their old, wilder feelings — without the need for chemical stimulation. But this doesn't happen overnight.

The first step on the road to enjoyable sober sex is to listen to your insides. If you're scared of having sex, allow yourself to be celibate for a while. If you shy away from intimate sex, perhaps friendly affairs are in order. If casual sex no longer suits you, hold out for meaningful sex. There's no best way to do it; the only goal is to meet your own needs.

When you do have sex, try to be in the moment and not to have expectations. If you're in a 12-step program, these pieces of advice will be familiar to you already, but they are still useful. Kathy says, "When I first started having sober sex, I grabbed at each sexual feeling and held on tight. The poor beaten-up feelings ran away from my stranglehold. Or else I'd boss my lovers around, trying to get them to give me the sensation I wanted, and *they'd* run away. But when I was willing to just feel what I was feeling, no matter how small, and ride through the times I lost the feelings, I found they came back, bigger and better. And while I *still* miss the orgasms I had with grass, my most complete physical and emotional sexual experiences have happened in the last couple of years, sober."

Rebecca had a similar experience: "I was afraid of going out on dates; everything that I would ordinarily have had a drink for — a first date, the first time sleeping with somebody — I had to do sober, which was very anxiety-producing. I even believed that my sexual pleasure wasn't worth the trouble; I wasn't getting that excited anymore. But, now, in this relationship — and it's happened to me before in sobriety — it's back to what it was."

There's no need to passively wait for time to pass to learn to enjoy sober sex. Therapy can help you deal with sexual inhibitions and fears. Keep a journal to discover who you are — and what you want from sex — clean and sober. Masturbating regularly will help you learn how you respond to stimulation without drugs or alcohol. Focus on the pleasure you feel rather than what you once felt or what you hope to feel in the future; in early sobriety, your sexual feelings may be subtle. Most importantly, be kind to yourself; rediscovering your sexuality is a form of exploration, not a test.

While it may be difficult to discuss sexual problems at 12-step meetings, private conversations with other people in recovery can be helpful, as they tell you how, like Kathy and Rebecca, they reclaimed their sexuality. And if the problems of sober sex should get too wearing, a 12-step meeting will remind you that having problems sober is still better than destroying your life abusing drugs and alcohol.

SPIRITUALITY. For some women, making love must be a spiritual experience or they feel the sex is meaningless. Other women just enjoy a good fuck. Neither belief system is better or more moral, though thousands of people are willing to insist that their way is the only way.

But what *is* a "spiritual sexual experience"? Like practically everything in sex, it's a matter of personal interpretation.

For Jessica, sexual spirituality is "just an intense connection with somebody. Not just a feeling of love but a feeling of overwhelming power, maybe awareness, a different sort of reality."

Lydia expresses her spirituality through her S/M practice: "The idea of power, giving up power, sharing power, plays into spirituality."

For Rebecca, "having sex with a woman is part of being in harmony with all living things. I feel like every time I make love with my lover, we're sending out all this positive, marvelous energy."

Suzanne says she and her lover "kid a lot about sex being a religious experience. There have been a lot of times, after making love, where the world looked different, and I felt cleansed and open. Good sex is celebratory. It can be ecstatic. It can be wacko. You speak in tongues. I can't think of a better way to be connected to the one you love and to the universe at large."

Realistically, no one reaches a transcendent level every time she has sex. Sexual spirituality is a goal, a gift, a blessing — not a requirement.

SPOONS. Just as sex can occur in many positions, so can cuddling. A favorite of many lesbians is "spoons."

Spooning offers full body contact with comfortable locations for both partners' arms and legs as you both lie on your sides facing in the same direction and the woman in back squishes up against the one in front. With one arm under her partner's neck, the woman in back can fully wrap her arms around the woman in front, and her head is at a perfect position for neck and shoulder kissing and nibbling. It's that simple, but it's also glorious.

STATISTICS. Since many lesbians are closeted, it's impossible to gather comprehensive and accurate statistics about lesbian habits and belief systems. Surveys of lesbians reveal data only about the women answering them; those women are self-selected from whatever small percentage of lesbians knew the survey existed in the first place.

Take Karla Jay and Allen Young's survey of 962 lesbians, as described in *The Gay Report* in 1977. In the table listing "respondents' source of questionnaire," entries include "friend," "political bookstore," "march or conference," "lesbian group," and "lesbian bar," among other similar locations. As a result, their survey focused on lesbians who frequented lesbian or feminist businesses or who had friends who did. Not surprisingly, the vast majority of respondents lived in cities, not rural areas.

Similarly, JoAnn Loulan s survey of 1,566 lesbians, as reported in 1987 in *Lesbian Passion*, described a limited pool of women, including those who went to her workshops and lectures and those who went to feminist bookstores or had friends who did.

These researchers acknowledged the limitations of their work. Jay and Young wrote, "We do not claim to have a scientific or representative sample of lesbians and gay men." Loulan referred to her "research on the lives and sex practices of *some* lesbians" [emphasis mine].

However, the information these researchers gathered is still valuable. Although the statistics cannot precisely delineate, for instance, exactly how many lesbians enjoy cunnilingus, they do provide a useful glimpse at the lesbian world. Through their findings, Jay and Young shattered the myth that lesbians are sexual paragons who always have orgasms, and Loulan discovered that some self-identified lesbians still have sex with men. Most importantly, these researchers broke the silence around lesbian sexuality, and the information they

gathered provided the first detailed pictures of who (some) lesbians are and what (some) lesbians are doing.

STRAIGHT WOMEN. It's not unusual for newly out lesbians to fall in love with straight women, particularly good friends whom they have loved for a *really* long time. And some lesbians, especially those who retain a mainstream idea of female beauty, may continue to fall in love with straight women. But it's an often painful habit.

Kathy's first love was her straight best friend: "We even made love once. We both enjoyed it, but I was ready to get married, while she went back to her boyfriend."

If a woman is really straight, lesbian sex won't completely satisfy her; though she may rave about your technique and sensitivity, she'll eventually want to sleep with a man. If you habitually fall in love with straight women, try going to lesbian meetings and activities where you can meet truly available women; you may also want to deal with any leftover internalized homophobia you feel. Or, should you decide that your attraction to straight women is too strong to give up, make your peace with loving women who invariably leave you.

But what if you suspect she isn't really straight? Maybe she flirts with you a lot. Well, she still may be straight; some heterosexual women flirt with lesbians instinctively, as they might flirt with men. But if she *is* a lesbian on the verge of coming out, you may devote months, even years, to helping her along. She may be confused; she may put one foot out the closet door and then pull it in again; or she may burst on out, thrilled with her freedom and with you. Once she is out, if indeed she does come out, she may stay with you, or not. The newly out woman needs to explore many options, and it is impossible to predict who she will be when she's done.

Because of this unpredictability, lesbian conventional wisdom warns against getting involved with newly out women. However, all relationships come without guarantees, so you might want to take a chance. Kathy knows a woman who waited two full years to see if the love of her life would come out of the closet; she did, and they've been together, happily ever after, for years. (See also *First Time; Internalized Homophobia.*)

SURVIVORS. Because of the prevalence of incest and rape, many lesbians are sexual abuse survivors. Many gay women also spend years in unhappy marriages, denying their real sexuality, which is another type of abuse. As a result, in most lesbian couples, at least one woman, and often both, are survivors of some form of sexual abuse. All but one of the women interviewed for this book are survivors.

Surviving sexual abuse has a tremendous impact on a woman's adult sex life. Few survivors are able to just relax into sex, with total trust for their partner and easy orgasms. Some women experience flashbacks of being molested or raped, and others find themselves overwhelmed with disturbing feelings. Jenn says, "At times, I don't like people to touch me, but not just sexually. Sometimes I don't even want people to bump into me or anything like that."

Survivors who have had easy sex with men may be surprised to find sex with women more difficult. Suzanne says, "After the rape, I kept my relationships with men safe through a variety of distancing techniques, but with women sex felt more dangerous. The distancing techniques just didn't work as well, since with women there's more intimacy. I feel like you can be quite safely alone when you're fucking with men, but women matter. Men haven't a clue what you're thinking or feeling. Women do. So it's more scary."

Healing. Many of the usual tools of sex, such as talking and openness, also aid survivors and their partners. However, survivors sometimes have trouble communicating fully; they may not be able to identify and express exactly what they are feeling, they may not want to make waves, and they may be frightened. Similarly, their partners may find communication awkward, particularly if they grow frustrated with sexual problems that seem to be the survivor's "fault" — and if they feel guilty for blaming the survivor. Both survivors and partners may find it difficult to balance their needs and fears.

Many survivors seek therapy, and there is a wealth of self-help books available, including *The Courage to Heal* and *Healing Your Sexual Self. Outgrowing the Pain* is a good first book to read as it offers an excellent, simple, highly readable overview of abuse. *Allies in Healing* focuses on partners.

Through therapy, self-help books, and their own imaginations, and with the help and support of their lovers, many survivors learn to relax and enjoy sex.

Jenn says, "If my lover touches me sexually and I shy away, she'll just hold me, and I calm down, because I feel very comfortable with her."

Gail is very careful whom she has sex with: "In my adult life, I've made the decision to not be sexual unless I want to be. I need a certain kind of woman who I feel I can trust with my body. I have to feel that she's going to be thoughtful. Then I still have to remind myself to relax and breathe and let go."

Suzanne uses self-talk to allow herself to enjoy sex: "When I'm making love with somebody or going to make love with somebody, I tell myself, 'You will still be there when this is over.' I can be very sexy when I know my lover is going away — because it's safe. But when there really is time to make love, part of me goes, eek, eek, and I want to run. So I tell myself, 'It's okay, this is now and this is her and you're going to like this.'"

SYMBOLS. Certain symbols have been embraced by the lesbian and gay community as our own. These symbols appear on publications, t-shirts, store windows, flyers, and jewelry. Wherever they are, they signal that "lesbians and gay men are here."

Freedom rings. Freedom rings were introduced at the 1991 San Francisco Freedom Day Parade. Designed by New York artist David Spada, the six anodized aluminum rings range in color from red to blue, forming a rainbow. They are worn on necklaces or keychains, as epaulets or bangles, or as finger rings. Later-generation designs have included "freedom triangles."

Labrys. The labrys is the double-headed ax of the Amazons. Used in jewelry and on t-shirts, the symbol does not include gay men.

Lambda. Originally adopted by the Gay Activists Alliance in the early 1970s, the Greek letter *lambda* now appears in the names of many lesbian and gay organizations. Some women feel that the lambda, which is the Greek equivalent of *L*, stands for *lesbian.*

Lavender. The association of lavender with homosexuality goes back thousands of years, and many lesbian- and gay-related posters, publications, t-shirts, and flyers are lavender.

Pink triangle. Probably the most universally used of the symbols, the pink triangle has its roots in the concentration camps of Nazi Germany. While Jews were forced to wear yellow Stars of David, gay men were forced to wear pink triangles with the point facing downward. Lesbians and gay men now wear pink triangles to announce "we are here" and "never again."
    There is some disputed evidence that lesbians were forced to wear black triangles in concentration camps; some contemporary lesbians have chosen black triangles over pink ones as their symbol.

Rainbow flag. Designed by Gilbert Baker of San Francisco in 1978, the rainbow flag is now a staple of gay pride marches and gatherings.

Women's symbols. Intertwined women's symbols often show up on lesbian t-shirts and earrings. For some reason, probably simplicity, they are also the symbols of choice for lesbian bathroom graffiti.

TEASING. Brush your fingers across the nape of her neck. Stroke her cheek with yours, mouths close, close, closer — but not quite touching. Lightly draw circles inside her palm with one fingertip. Ignore her erotic centers — breasts, mouth, vulva — until she's ready to explode. Then kiss her, or stroke her labia, or suck her nipples, and she *will* explode.

You get the idea.

One of Kathy's fondest memories includes extended teasing: "We knew we were going to sleep together for the first time that night, and we were dying to start, but we stayed at the Meg Christian concert and played with each other's hands for two hours. Toward the end of the concert, I kissed the side of her head and she moaned out loud. Afterward, we ran home and had lovely sex. The next morning, when we discussed the concert, we laughed and laughed; neither of us could remember a single song Meg played."

THERAPY. Since the world is saturated with homophobia, virtually all lesbians reach adulthood scarred and suffering from at least some self-hate. In addition, many gay women are incest or rape survivors or recovering alcoholics and addicts. No wonder many seek help from therapists at some point in their lives.

But choosing a therapist poses a particular challenge to lesbians, both as women and as homosexuals. Too many therapists are sexist, homophobic, or just clueless about lesbians. Alice's first therapist was pleased because she happened to wear a skirt; he congratulated her on her "adjustment to heterosexuality." When Suzanne told a school psychologist she had been raped, he asked why she was trying to avoid taking responsibility for having sex.

Rebecca's story includes the good, the bad, and the ugly: "I had fourteen years with a Freudian therapist, who told me it was wonderful I felt guilty about masturbating because the guilt would help me to stop. He said nothing but sexual intercourse was normal, and he told me, 'Forget about being homosexual, you're not.' He did tremendous damage. In his office, I was defined as frigid; I wasn't defined as a lesbian. So I worked on my frigidity for fourteen years. That was very debilitating. But now, years later, I'm doing inner-child work with a different therapist, and I'm getting in touch with the spontaneous emotional part of myself. I was always in touch with my hurt and anger but not my better parts. Maybe it's because of the work I'm doing with this therapist that I am enjoying sex so much more recently."

Although gay women can receive good therapy from straight people, lesbian therapists have a deep personal understanding of what it means to be gay and female. Kathy stopped going to a straight woman although she helped Kathy to quit smoking pot, because, "it's easier to get to the deeper stuff when you don't have to explain the basics first." Alice, on the other hand, is totally pleased with her straight female therapist, and a friend of hers receives excellent therapy from a gay man.

And, yes, lesbians can have therapeutic success with straight male therapists, but they have to be *exceptional* straight male therapists. Be careful if you take this route, or you may find yourself having to educate him before he can help you — if he's educable.

The best way to find a therapist is through personal recommendations, so ask your friends who they go to. If you live in an area with a lesbian and gay center or hotline, see if there is a referral service available for gay and gay-friendly therapists.

When seeking a therapist, lesbian or otherwise, prepare a list of questions. Ask about her background and degrees. Social workers use different techniques than analysts, who have different goals than psychiatrists, who don't always agree with psychologists, who view therapy differently than do psychiatric nurses. Ask about her attitude toward homosexuality. Does she prescribe drugs? Is she goal-oriented? Is therapy to be long-term or short-term? Does she have any other lesbian patients? If possible, have sessions with four or five therapists before making a choice.

Sometimes you will be uncomfortable during therapy because of dealing with difficult emotions, but if you become seriously disturbed about your therapist herself, trust your instincts. If you believe your therapist has her own agenda, such as "curing" your homosexuality, or if you think she's weird, or if you just don't like her, get a new therapist! Don't worry about being "wrong" or "right"; even if the therapist is compassionate and brilliant, she is not right for you if she makes you tense and ill at ease.

Stop seeing any therapist who makes sexual moves on you. That's never acceptable. *Never.* Report her to whatever governing board is appropriate. (If you're not sure where to report the abuse, call another therapist and ask. You don't have to name names; just say that you want to report a case of misconduct.)

THREESOMES. Imagine two women licking your nipples at the same time. Or one woman kissing you while another goes down on you. If you're into threesomes, they can be heavenly. Lydia's threesomes have ranged "from very good to okay." Kathy says, "I tried threesomes twice;

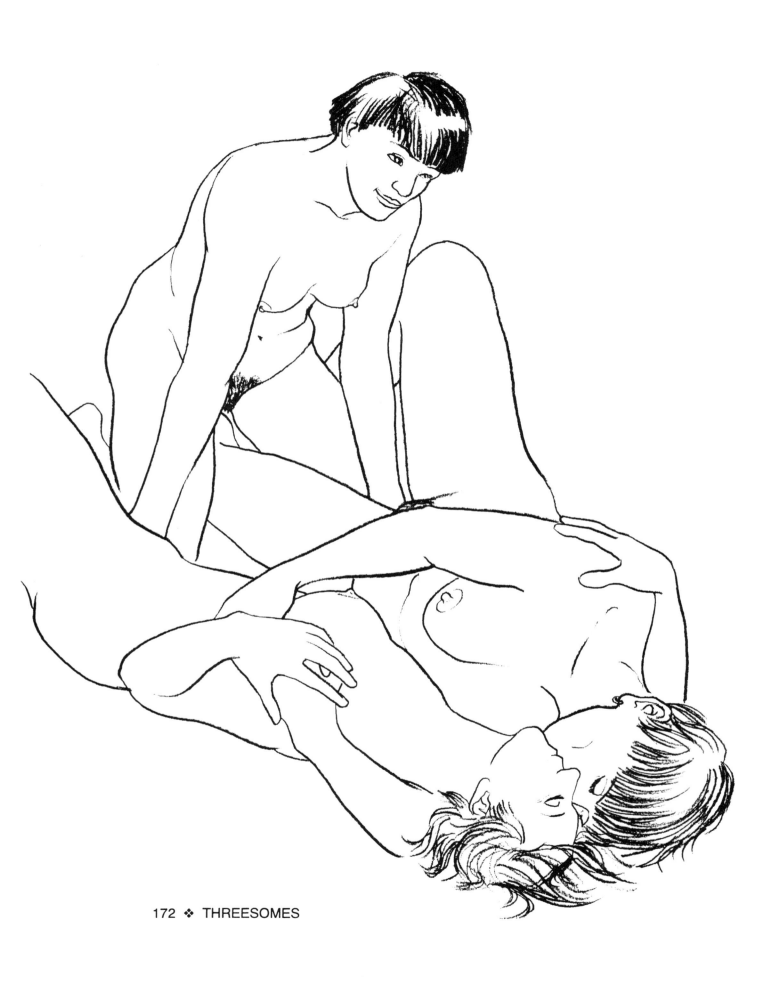

once was great fun, once was terrible." Jenn holds a different point of view: "I don't really enjoy threesomes, because that's not enough people."

The first ingredient required for a successful threesome is honesty, particularly if two women in a relationship choose to have sex with a third woman. How will the couple keep their boundaries intact? Do they want to? Is one partner just going along to please her lover?

You can't necessarily predict how it will feel to watch your girlfriend kissing someone else. You may experience more jealousy than you ever anticipated — or more passion! You might even become annoyed if your lover *doesn't* get jealous watching you kiss someone else.

If the threesome comprises three single women, jealousy can still be an issue. What if two of the women hit it off and the third gets left out?

Because of the difficulties inherent in threesomes, they are not that frequent among lesbians. But if you do choose to participate in one, there are a million things you all can do together. You can take turns making each woman the center of incredible amounts of attention. You can form a daisy chain as woman A goes down on B who goes down on C who goes down on A. Or, if A and B are lying face-to-face, kissing and rubbing, C can squat down between their legs and penetrate both of them at the same time. Or two of you can sandwich the third between you, kissing her neck and shoulders and mouth and burying her in sensation.

With honesty, fairness, imagination, and an open mind, a threesome can be an experience to remember forever. (See also *Group Sex.*)

TIME OF DAY. Mention morning sex to two women. One says, "What a great way to begin the day"; the other talks of morning breath and crud-caked eyes. The best time of day to make love is a personal preference. If you and your lover have differing preferences, take turns.

Unfortunately, some lesbians' favorite times are co-opted by work and school or taking care of the kids. A few of the women interviewed for this book expressed a desire for afternoon sex but added that it's rarely possible in their lives. How sad that so many people can only fit sex in after the bills are paid and the errands are run!

Nevertheless, if you're suffering from a habit-deadened sex life, try making a pass at your lover at an unexpected moment. Put those dishes aside, do the shopping later, tape the TV show, and give her a long kiss. It may be just the thing to jump-start your love life.

TOUCH. One of the transcendent joys of lesbian sex is simply touching another woman. Stroke her back firmly with the whole palm of your hand, from her shoulders to her butt. Or teasingly pet the back of her

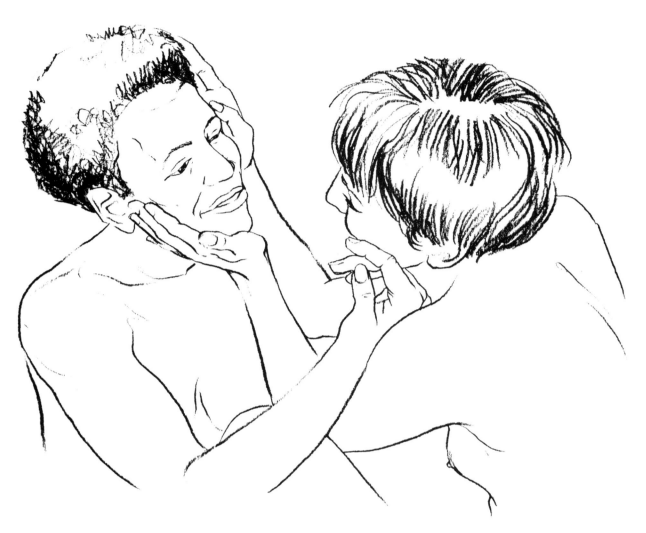

neck with one finger. Caress her cheek with the backs of your fingers and then with your whole hand. Run your hair along her breasts and belly. Brush your lips across her shoulders and neck. Knead her biceps or thighs. Rub your breasts down her back or circle her breasts with your own. Draw your hands slowly down her sides. Vary strokes, firmness, and direction, or use one finger to explore her whole body. Each touch produces different, lovely sensations for her — and for you.

Remember: skin is the largest sex organ.

TOYS. Almost anything can be a sex toy. Try feathers or different materials for stroking; leather, silk, cotton, felt, flannel, and terrycloth each excite a unique sensation. Dildos and vegetables are great for penetration; blindfolds and bondage add a frisson of danger and mystery to sex. A kitchen apron becomes a sex toy when worn with nothing else. Use your sexual imagination while searching around your house, and those quotidian household items may never look the same.

TRIBADISM. The word *tribade* (pronounced *trib*-id), another name for *lesbian*, comes from the Greek for "she who rubs," and *tribadism* (*trib*-i-diz-im) is the practice of sexual rubbing, or humping. The words are unpopular because they're ugly and unfamiliar. Suzanne says, "Tribadism sounds too much like arachnophobia or something," and Jessica says, "When I first read about tribadism, I thought it meant I had to do three things at once."

Few lesbians, if any, use the word *tribadism* seriously; don't expect anyone to say to you, "Hey, baby, wanna tribadate?" Nor will they often say, "Wanna hump?" Tribadism occurs naturally when two women lie down (whether one on top of the other or face-to-face on their sides) or dance together. Hips move, pelvises grind, breasts mush together — and, voila, tribadism occurs.

Although tribadism has been described as a "desperate attempt at heterosexuality" (please!) by the very ignorant, mutual undulation is a juicily delightful lesbian thang. What could be more lesbian than hot wet labia slipping and sliding on each other's thighs as you roll together? If your anatomies are compatible, you may also achieve direct labia-to-labia and clitoris-to-clitoris contact. It's all truly heavenly!

If you'd like, add variety to your life as a tribade; clitoris-to-elbow, clitoris-to-kneecap, and clitoris-to-shoulder rubbing all have their charms, and all can lead to orgasm.

If you've never had a tribadal orgasm and want one, experiment with different positions until you achieve the stimulation you desire. Try rubbing together, legs entwined, each with a vulva against the other's thigh — or pubic bone to pubic bone. You may receive more stimulation when you're on top — or on the bottom. Perhaps you will prefer tribadating on your side, face-to-face with your partner. Your comfort and excitement will depend on your personal anatomy, and the research affords its own fun — not to mention an excellent aerobic workout.

If you fail to reach orgasm through tribadism, but you crave coming face-to-face with your partner, stick a vibrator between you and let *it* do the work.

TRUST. Trust is hard to grow and easy to destroy. Treat trust carefully; once it's been broken, it may never be fixed. Don't assume you trust somebody immediately; you probably don't, nor should you. Trust takes time, and a little caution is a wonderful thing.

When establishing trust, two factors come into play: the behavior of the current loved one and the behavior of all the loved ones in the past, including family members. Women who have been abused will be particularly slow to trust a new lover.

Suzanne says, "One of the biggest trust builders for me is the sense that somebody's willing to be patient, so if I'm feeling nervous or afraid, it's okay. Flexibility and caring are important both in the relationship and in making love." For Lydia, "shared experience builds trust — knowing someone over time and knowing that they're consistently honest, that they're consistently willing to be open and to be supportive."

Some women may find that they need to stop occasionally or that they freeze up during sex. If the woman they are with loses patience with them, their tentative trust disappears and they cannot continue. But if the woman is supportive and loving, holding them quietly for a while, they generally can get back into the experience, and true trust starts growing.

Trust-busters are many; dishonesty, infidelity, and unreliability are three biggies.

Interestingly enough, some lesbians can have good sex — even great sex — with women they don't trust, but it gets exhausting. (See also *Jealousy.*)

TYPES. Lesbians by and large don't go for specific "types." The same woman may date big women and small, old women and young, flat-topped and corn-rowed. When the women interviewed for this book were asked what they looked for in other women, they named personality attributes ("self-assertive," "enjoys sex," "strong," "has a good attitude") more frequently than physical ones ("butch," "femme," "soft butch," "muscle-y," "clean"). Not one listed size, shape, age, and color requirements. (See also *Appearances; Butch/Femme; Cultural Differences.*)

V–Z

VAGINAL ORGASMS. Once upon a time, Sigmund Freud decided that vaginal orgasms were "more mature" than clitoral orgasms. He initiated years of misery for women by claiming they were frigid or immature unless they achieved orgasm through penile-vaginal intercourse.

Decades later, after much damage had been done in Freud's name, feminists and modern sex researchers announced that vaginal orgasms are a myth. More recently, biologist Stephen Jay Gould devoted a chapter of his *Bully for Brontosaurus* to explaining the evolutionary reasons why vaginal orgasms are physically *impossible.* All orgasms are clitoral in origin, even those that occur during penetration; although some orgasms *seem* to come from penetration itself, they actually arise from the clitoris getting rubbed and manipulated between the partners' bodies.

This is where women go "whew" and wipe our brows, right? After years of being told our sexuality was second-rate, we've been relieved of the need to seek vaginal orgasms. They simply don't exist. Right?

Just one problem: lots of women have them!

Rebecca's experience covers the gamut from Freud to freedom: "The joke of my life is that I spent fourteen years in therapy trying to have a vaginal orgasm when I was straight. Then I came out into the movement, and everybody said there's no such thing. I felt really ripped off because I had been trying to have one for all the years of my marriage, but I also felt relief. I figured, okay, never have to think about that again. Well, the first time I had one with a woman, I think I laughed for forty minutes. I don't know if I was laughing or crying, but I was hysterical."

Lydia states simply, "I know there are vaginal orgasms because I have them," and Jessica says, "It's a very different feeling to come just with my clitoris than to come just with my vagina." However, Gail says, "I don't know if I could really say that there's a clitoral and a vaginal orgasm. I think the whole area is being stimulated." Suzanne agrees: "It's all connected."

Are these physical differences or semantic ones? If an orgasm results from stimulation of the G-spot or the entire vagina, it's a vaginal orgasm, right? But *A New View of a Woman's Body* defines the whole genital area as part of the clitoris! So a vaginal orgasm *is* a clitoral orgasm.

Maybe.

Don't worry about labels. There's no single right way to have an orgasm and there's certainly no *wrong* way to have one. (Lydia says orgasms are like kittens: "How can you not be fond of a kitten? How can you not be fond of an orgasm?")

If you're happy with your orgasms as they are, that's what counts. Don't get bogged down in correct locations or specific definitions or Freudian or feminist interpretations. Someday, maybe, scientists and sex researchers will agree about orgasms and where they come from, but the information won't make the orgasms feel any different.

If, however, you're not happy with your orgasms, or don't have orgasms, or have clitoral orgasms only and want to experience vaginal orgasms, there are ways for you to achieve more sexual satisfaction. First, start practicing. Try a vibrator with a special G-spot attachment; vibrators provide strong, consistent, and reliable stimulation. Do daily Kegel exercises to strengthen the muscles that spasm during orgasm. Try new angles, more foreplay, and erotica. Rather than focusing on the potential orgasm, enjoy whatever feelings you experience as they happen. With patience and practice, you can improve your sexual response radically.

And give yourself a break now and then; sometimes taking time off will improve your response. Jessica says, "If I know I'm going to sleep with somebody, I won't have sex for a week with myself or anybody, because I love to have vaginal orgasms, and they are harder to have. So I'll store up energy." (See also *Sexual Growth.*)

VANILLA SEX. (Non-S/M sex.)

As you start exploring lesbian sex publications, you may conclude that all lesbians are into S/M and watersports and anal sex and various other practices that simply don't appeal to you. You may feel pressured to try these forms of sex just to fit in. But many, many, many lesbians are thrilled with their totally vanilla sex lives. S/M and other alternative practices fill lesbian sex books and magazines because S/M women were some of the first lesbians to start talking about sex, and they invented a thriving sex industry to meet their needs. But these publications do not represent all gay women.

If you want to limit your sex reading to more vanilla topics, see collections such as *Bushfire* and the lesbian romantic novels put out by Naiad Press. There is plenty of vanilla sex writing around.

VEGETABLES. When using veggies as "Mother Nature's dildos," also use common sense. Feel them carefully for minute hairs or scratchy parts. Clean them thoroughly before use; if there's any chance they have chemicals on them, soak them in soapy water or use a condom.

Don't use veggies straight from the fridge unless you *want* that ice-cold sensation in your vagina. Steaming a carrot can warm it without making it squishy; leaving a cucumber in the sun all day will make it more flexible but still firm enough to use.

If you are planning to purchase a dildo, experiment with various-sized veggies to ascertain what diameter meets your needs most consistently. Trying a wrong-sized cuke will cost you sixty-five cents; trying a wrong-sized dildo could cost you thirty-five dollars.

VIBRATORS. Vibrators (or "personal massagers," as the mainstream brands are known) provide a strong, steady, rhythmical pressure that almost guarantees orgasm. From the industrial-sized wands to the penis-shaped cheapies, vibrators can add great pleasure to sex, whether with a partner or solo. (Note: most battery-operated vibrators are considerably weaker and less reliable than plug-in-the-wall models.)

Vibrators make easily orgasmic women come in minutes — or seconds. For women who are preorgasmic, vibrators provide nonstop stimulation and eliminate the worry about a lover's fingers or tongue falling off. It's never necessary to ask a vibrator, "Am I taking too long?"

Some women like to use vibrators right on their clits, while others use a blanket or their labia majora to provide a cushion. Vibrators vary in intensity, so be careful when first playing with a new one, then listen to your body. Kathy warns, "I found out the hard way that it's not a good idea to hold your vibrator near its on/off switch when masturbating. One night, my hand clenched as I started to come, *and I turned off the vibrator.* I was pretty pissed, let me tell you."

Be cautious when using a vibrator internally. If you're not sure your vibrator is safe for vaginal use, call the manufacturer, Good Vibrations, or Eve's Garden for advice (see the *Resource List*). Attachments designed specifically for internal use exist for some types of vibrators, including curved devices ideal for G-spot stimulation. Again, contact Good Vibrations or Eve's Garden for more information.

A myth prevails in the lesbian world that vibrator use is addicting and that, after habitual vibrator use, orgasm from oral or digital sex is no longer possible. No one has produced any proof that this occurs, but if you are worried, vary your sexual habits. Use fingers sometimes, tongues sometimes, and vibrators sometimes. Or start with your vibrator and finish with your fingers — or vice versa. If your orgasm feels less intense when induced manually, add more foreplay or read some erotica. Or take a day or a week off from coming.

Kathy loves masturbating with her vibrator and says, "I usually keep it next to my bed. When I feel I'm using it too often, I put it in a closet for a while, and I find I'm not addicted, I'm just lazy. When the vibrator's not right there, I masturbate manually and have a grand old time."

In a past relationship, Alice and her lover would lie face-to-face with a wand vibrator between them as they kissed and rocked together. They used this position so often that Alice was afraid that she'd never come any other way. In her next relationship, she rediscovered oral and digital sex and came with no problem.

So go ahead and use your vibrator; you'll probably have years of fun without needing a Vibrators Anonymous meeting. Gail has five vibrators, and her sex life is just fine, thank you.

Oh, yeah; vibrators are great for massages too.

VOCABULARY. What do you call the place between a lesbian's thighs?

"I guess I say *pussy*," is Suzanne's answer. "I don't like *cunt* 'cause it sounds hard. *Vulva* sounds clinical."

"*Cunt* or *her*," says Jessica. "*Pussy* sounds too silly and reminds me of what men say."

"*Vagina*," says Gail.

"*Pussy* or *twat*," says Kathy. "Or whatever my lover uses."

"I'm not comfortable with words like *pussy*," says Rebecca. "I would probably say *crotch*. Or 'in between your legs' — that's what I'd be happiest with."

"I usually say *cunt*," answers Lydia. "*Twat* doesn't feel right. I use *vagina* to distinguish that part of the vulva, the cunt, whatever, from the rest of it."

"*Heaven*," says Alice.

During the interviews, the only woman who sounded totally pleased with her answer was Alice. *No* existing word completely fills the need for a positive, sexy, euphonious name for women's wonderful genitals. Formal words are too ... formal. And slang words often carry uncomfortable associations from past experiences with men in bed or on the street. (Although English is renowned for its extensive vocabulary, it often fails when it comes to sex: try to come up with one positive word that names an adult woman, unmarried, who enjoys making love.)

The vocabulary choices for oral sex aren't too bad. While *cunnilingus* has limited use in bed ("Oh baby, oh baby, please perform cunnilingus on me!"), "please go down on me" and "lick me" get the point across quite nicely. Penetration can be requested with a lovely "please come inside me" or "put your fingers in me," although many lesbians prefer the old-fashioned, Anglo-Saxon "fuck me!" (Keep in mind, however, that lesbians who dislike the word *fuck* tend to dislike it vehemently.)

So, it's your first time having sex with a particular woman. You don't know if she prefers *vagina, cunt,* or *pussy*. You haven't a clue whether *fuck* will turn her on or off. You're not even sure if you can pronounce *cunnilingus*. How do you find out which words she prefers?

Ask her!

Timing is important, of course. Does it really matter what you call a *pussy, twat,* or *cunt* when you have one in your mouth? But, when the moment seems right, a little investigation will go a long way. Not only can you gain information, but you can also make the conversation itself sexy. Stroke or kiss the various places you'd like her to name. While on a date, whisper sex words to each other in a restaurant over a meal of artichokes or sushi. If you're into fantasy, have one of you be an English professor teaching a vocabulary lesson.

And, as in all things sexual, give each other some slack. If she yells out a word that offends you in the midst of passion, remember, *she's in the midst of passion.* It's a good time for her to keep the editor of her mind turned off. On the other hand, if a word so alienates you as to ruin your sexual experience, maybe the next time she can leave the mental editor on just the slightest bit. These sorts of compromises lead to more trust and better sex.

Many lesbians invent their own vocabularies. *Bouncing* provides more fun than the awful *tribadism; self-sex* and *petting the bunny* sound warmer than *masturbation.* Suzanne and her lover reshape existing slang or reclaim negative words, usually with a personal twist. Kathy and her lover tend toward permutations of vocabulary from other languages. Alice finds that words practically invent themselves if she just listens to what she's feeling. All prefer their own words to the limited ones offered by English.

WATER. Water is one of those sex specialties that is occasionally wonderful and occasionally more trouble than it's worth.

Some women like to masturbate by holding their vulvas under the faucet in the bathtub. But Suzanne says, "Mostly it was just hideously uncomfortable and the bathtub was too small and I felt like I was going to drown at the top of the tub." Shower massages offer more angles and a better way to stimulate your clitoris without drowning, but they can be maddeningly too short to reach you where you want them to. If you do have the right shower massage and you're ready to go, be careful; shooting water up your vagina can damage your insides.

If you tend to get weak-kneed when you come, make sure you can sit while masturbating in the tub, or perhaps stick to a safer method. And be careful if you try oral sex in the shower; you may find that gallons of water drip off of her belly right into your mouth and nose!

All caveats aside, water orgasms can be wonderful. If your body size and shape allow it, running the faucet on your clit can give you a delicious come, and shower massages offer vibratorlike consistency and speed. Even touching yourself in the bathtub can be special, as you bask in warm wetness. Depending on your size and shape, the sides of the tub may restrict your usual spasms and thereby intensify your orgasm.

Bathing together can be lovely once you figure out where to put your elbows and knees and how to deal with faucets in your back. Showering together is simpler, but still lovely. While you wash each other, slide your hands along her beautiful skin. Watch the water drip down her breasts and nipples. As you scrub her back, kiss the water that flows over her shoulders. And when you're done, dry each other lovingly, slowly, thoroughly. It's great foreplay.

One other use for water utilizes its coldest form. Hold a small piece of ice in your mouth as you go down on her. If she doesn't hate it, she may well love it!

WEIGHT. See *Body Image.*

WHAT DO WOMEN WANT? Sigmund Freud once wrote that, after thirty years of research into the "feminine soul," he still could not answer, "What does a woman want?" Even the question reveals ignorance, using the singular as though it were possible to codify one set of desires that characterizes all women, but at least Freud *knew* he was clueless.

From Freud's time through the 1960s, men continued to try to psych out women, writing serious tomes on their feeble findings. Not that long ago, even books on female sexuality and female orgasms were all written by men. "Vaginal orgasms are more mature than clitoral ones," they wrote. Or, "Although women can have splendid orgasms, they don't really need them; they just want to be cuddled." Or, as the sexual revolution began, "Although many women are multiorgasmic, one orgasm is usually enough for a woman." That generous allowance of one orgasm per woman per sex act showed progress in sex writing!

Then came feminism, and women started talking for ourselves. From Shere Hite to Susie Bright, from Erica Jong to Pat Califia, from Nancy Friday to JoAnn Loulan, women revealed a landscape of sexual desires including mountains, valleys, rivers, oceans, deserts, forests, and some topographical features that have yet to be named. Through this writing came the answer to Freud's question. What do women want? Everything — at least sexually.

Although not every woman desires every experience every day, women want lovemaking and down-and-dirty sex, cuddling and bondage, monogamy and promiscuity, women and men, fluttery kisses and serious fucking, celibacy and constant sex, to take and be taken.

It's simple, really: women, particularly lesbians, want and demand the freedom to express ourselves sexually when we wish, in the manner we choose, without the interference of church, government, or prevailing prejudices.

That's what women want.

WHO'S ON TOP? When people ask lesbian couples, "Who's the man?" they're really asking, "Who's on top?" or, "Who's fucking whom?" — a question that comes from a totally heterosexist perspective. Most lesbians take turns being on top, bottom, and side to side. In addition, the assumption that the person on top is the doer, while the person on the bottom is done to, goes out the window in the reality of lesbian sex. (See *Positions.*)

This is not to say that there aren't couples who follow strict roles in bed. The no-touch butch is not extinct, and many S/M couples follow carefully defined rules. But there are also butch bottoms and aggressive femmes and all sorts of combinations in between. The most masculine-looking woman may be too shy to make a pass, and the littlest femme may be commanding in bed.

Lesbians don't go through all the trouble of coming out in order to re-create the limitations of heterosexual sex.

RESOURCE LIST

CHILDREN'S BOOKS

The Duke Who Outlawed Jelly Beans and Other Stories, by Johnny Valentine, illustrated by Lynette Schmidt (Alyson Wonderland, 1991). Five fairy tales about kids with lesbian or gay parents.

Gloria Goes to Gay Pride, by Lesléa Newman, illustrated by Russell Crocker (Alyson Wonderland, 1991). Young Gloria goes to gay pride with her two moms.

Heather Has Two Mommies, by Lesléa Newman, illustrated by Diana Souza (Alyson Wonderland, 1991). A story about a three-year-old daughter of lesbian moms.

EROTICA

Bad Attitude, P.O. Box 390110, Cambridge, MA 02139; (508) 372-6277. Hard-core lesbian sex magazine full of fiction, photos, and S/M.

Bushfire, edited by Karen Barber (Alyson Publications, 1991). Collected lesbian erotic fiction.

Curious Wine, by Katherine Forrest (Naiad, 1983). A charming coming-out novel, filled with hot vanilla sex.

Macho Sluts, by Pat Califia (Alyson Publications, 1988). Hard-core S/M stories, including group sex and adventures with men.

The Poetry of Sex, edited by Tee Corinne (Banned Books, 1992). Lesbian erotic poetry.

Serious Pleasure, edited by the Sheba Collective (Cleis, 1989). Lesbian erotic stories and poetry.

Wanting Women, edited by Jan Hardy (Sidewalk Revolution Press, 1990). Lesbian erotic poetry.

HISTORY

Alyson Almanac (Alyson Publications, 1990). Includes an overview of lesbian and gay history, brief biographies of historical queers, and much other information.

Odd Girls and Twilight Lovers, by Lillian Faderman (Penguin, 1991). A history of lesbian life in the United States in the twentieth century.

The Persistent Desire, edited by Joan Nestle (Alyson Publications, 1992). More than sixty women trace the history and meaning of butch/femme roles throughout this century. Inspiring, moving, painful, important.

A Restricted Country, by Joan Nestle (Firebrand Books, 1987). Writings on lesbian life in the 1950s and 1960s, sexual politics, and sex.

Why Can't Sharon Kowalski Come Home? by Karen Thompson and Julie Andrzejewski (Spinsters/Aunt Lute, 1988). When Karen Thompson's lover Sharon Kowalski was seriously injured in a car accident, Kowalski's parents became her guardians and Thompson was forbidden even to visit her. This book follows Thompson's fight to live with and take care of the woman she loves.

MAIL ORDER

Alyson Publications, 40 Plympton Street, Boston, MA 02118; (617) 542-5679. Publishes fiction and nonfiction for lesbians (as well as gay men, bisexuals, and children), including *Bushfire, Coming to Power, The Persistent Desire*, and this book.

Blush Entertainment, 536 Castro Street, San Francisco, CA 94114; (800) 845-4617. Sells erotic videos, made by and for lesbians.

Cleis Press, P.O. Box 14684, San Francisco, CA 94114. Publishes lesbian fiction, nonfiction, and erotica.

A Different Light Bookstore, (800) 343-4002; in NYC, call (212) 989-4850. Lesbian and gay bookstore, located in New York, San Francisco, and West Hollywood. Mail-order department offers "any lesbian/gay book in print."

Down There Press/Yes Press, 938 Howard Street, San Francisco, CA 94103; (415) 974-8985. Publishes female (not exclusively lesbian) erotica.

Eve's Garden, 119 West 57th Street, Suite 420, New York, NY 10019; (212) 757-8651. Sells vibrators, dildos, lubricants, safe-sex supplies, books on sexual pleasure and health, erotic literature for and by women, and more. Charges $3.00 for catalogue.

Firebrand Books, 141 The Commons, Ithaca, NY 14850. Publishes lesbian fiction, nonfiction, and erotica.

Frederick's of Hollywood, (800) 323-9525. Famous purveyor of sexy clothing.

Good Vibrations, Open Enterprises, 1210 Valencia Street, San Francisco, CA 94110. Sells vibrators, dildos, lubricants, safe-sex supplies, books on sexual pleasure and health, erotic literature for and by women, videos, and more. Charges $4 for each of two catalogues, one of books and videos and the other of sex toys and supplies, or $5 for both (fee good toward first order).

Lambda Rising, 1625 Connecticut Avenue, NW, Washington, DC 20009; (800) 621-6969. Lesbian and gay bookstore with three locations and phone-fax-mail order service. Stocks in-print and out-of-print books as well as videos, music, jewelry, and greeting cards.

Lane Bryant, (800) 477-7070. Clothing for large women; includes sexy underwear.

Naiad Press, Box 10543, Tallahassee, FL 32302; (904) 539-5965. Lesbian publisher: specializes in lesbian genre fiction, including erotica, westerns, mysteries, romances, and science fiction.

Sapphile, Old Chelsea Station, P.O. Box 1274, New York, NY 10113-0920. Periodically sends out lesbian- and gay-related mailings, including info on merchandise, magazines, books, and services.

Stormy Leather, 1158 Howard Street, San Francisco, CA 94103; (415) 626-1672. A source for leather wear, restraints, and other sex toys.

Victoria's Secret, (800) HER-GIFT. A source of very sexy underwear and nightwear; their ads look like soft-core porn.

OTHER

The Art of Erotic Massage, by Andrew Yorke (Blandford, 1988). Filled with great techniques, but hyper-heterosexual.

The Beauty Myth: How Images of Beauty Are Used against Women, by Naomi Wolf (Anchor Books, 1992). An exploration of how the media train women to be dissatisfied with their bodies.

"The Bonobos' Peaceable Kingdom," by Takayoshi Kano. *Natural History* magazine, November 1990. A discussion of bonobos by a researcher who has been studying them since 1974.

Bully for Brontosaurus: Reflections in Natural History, by Stephen Jay Gould (Norton, 1991). The chapter "Male Nipples and Clitoral Ripples" discusses the biological reasons women cannot have vaginal orgasms (!).

"No Evidence for Female-to-Female HIV Transmission among 960,000 Female Blood Donors," by Lyle R. Petersen, Lynda Doll, Carol White, Susan Chu, and the HIV Blood Donor Study Group. *Journal of Acquired Immune Deficiency Syndromes,* 1992, Vol. 5, No. 9, pp. 853–855.

"Risky Business: Should Lesbians Practice Safer Sex?" by Nancy Solomon. *Out/Look,* Spring 1992, pp. 47–52.

With the Power of Each Breath, edited by Susan E. Browne, Debra Connors, and Nanci Stern (Cleis Press, 1985). An anthology of writings by and about women with disabilities; topics range from "surviving the system" to "the body I love."

Write from the Heart: Lesbians Healing from Heartache, edited by Anita L. Pace (Baby Steps Press, 1992). Lesbians write about recovering from breakups.

SELF-HELP

Alcoholics Anonymous, General Service Office, P.O. Box 459, Grand Central Station, New York, NY 10163; (212) 870-3400.

Alive and Well, by Cuca Hepburn with Bonnie Gutierrez (Crossing Press, 1988). A useful but highly opinionated lesbian health guide, with everything from finding a doctor to calcium-rich foods. Argues that S/M is unhealthy.

Allies in Healing: When the Person You Love Was Sexually Abused as a Child, by Laura Davis (Harper Perennial, 1991). A self-help book for partners of abuse survivors; not specifically aimed at lesbians, but gay-aware.

Asian Health Project, 3860 West Martin Luther King Boulevard, Los Angeles, CA 90008; (213) 295-6571.

The Change: Women, Aging and the Menopause, by Germaine Greer (Knopf, 1992). Germaine Greer takes on menopause.

Coming Out: An Act of Love, by Rob Eichberg (Plume, 1991). A general coming-out guide.

Coming Out to Parents: A Two-Way Survival Guide for Lesbians and Gay Men and Their Parents, by Mary V. Borhek (Pilgrim, 1983). Ways to smooth out the coming-out process for both the lesbian or gay man and the parents.

Considering Parenthood, by Cheri Pies (Spinsters, 1985). A comprehensive guide to lesbian parenthood, including the medical, emotional, and legal ramifications of having and adopting children.

The Courage to Heal, by Ellen Bass and Laura Davis (Harper & Row, 1988). An expansive and detailed exploration of how to heal from childhood abuse, specifically for "women survivors of child sexual abuse." Very lesbian-aware.

The Final Closet: The Gay Parents' Guide for Coming Out to Their Children, by Rip Corley (Editech Press, 1990). Good advice, with a clinical bent.

Healing Your Sexual Self, by Janet G. Woititz (Health Communications, 1989). For adults abused as children who have trouble with sex and intimacy.

A Legal Guide for Lesbian and Gay Couples, by Hayden Curry and Denis Clifford (Nolo Press Self-Help Law, 1991). Provides detailed guidelines and sample paperwork for wills, living-together contracts, co-parenting arrangements, and more. Make sure to get the most recent edition, as laws change frequently.

Lesbians at Midlife: The Creative Transition, edited by Barbara Sang, Joyce Warshow, and Adrienne J. Smith (Spinsters, 1991). A many-authored anthology covering topics from "embracing changes" to "rediscovering our creativity and spirituality."

Ms. magazine, 230 Park Avenue, New York, NY 10169; (212) 551-9595.

Naming the Violence: Speaking Out about Lesbian Battering, edited by Kerry Lobel for the National Coalition Against Domestic Violence Lesbian Task Force (Seal Press, 1986). A general overview of battering in lesbian relationships, including personal experiences, social ramifications, and the availability of support for battered lesbians, written by survivors and domestic violence workers.

National Black Women's Health Project, 1237 Ralph Abernathy Boulevard, SW, Atlanta, GA 30310; (404) 758-9590 or (800) ASK-BWHP.

National Latina Health Organization, P.O. Box 7567, Oakland, CA 94601; (510) 534-1362.

National Women's Health Network, 1325 G Street, NW, Washington, DC 20005; (202) 347-1140.

Native American Women's Health Education Resource Center, P.O. Box 572, Lake Andes, SD 57356; (605) 487-7072.

The New Our Bodies, Ourselves, by the Boston Women's Health Book Collective (Simon & Schuster, 1992). General information about women's health and social issues, regularly updated, with some focus on lesbians.

A New View of a Woman's Body, by the Federation of Feminist Women's Health Centers (Feminist Health Press, 1991). Includes a liberating re-evaluation of female genitalia.

Ourselves, Growing Older, by Paula Brown Doress and Diana Laskin Siegal and the Midlife and Older Women Book Project (Simon & Schuster, 1987). All about women and aging, including such topics as menopause, medical problems, sexuality, and relationship issues, with some focus on lesbians.

Outgrowing the Pain, by Eliana M. Gill (Launch Press, 1984). Subtitled "A Book for and about Adults Abused as Children"; reader-friendly and nonintimidating.

Permanent Partners: Building Gay and Lesbian Relationships That Last, by Betty Berzon (Dutton, 1988). How to achieve "happily ever after."

The Rights of Lesbians and Gay Men: The Basic ACLU Guide to a Gay Person's Rights, by Nan D. Hunter, Sherryl E. Michaelson, and Thomas B. Stoddard (Southern Illinois University Press, 1992). Includes information on lesbian and gay rights pertinent to employment, housing, the military, families, and criminal law.

Secular Organizations for Sobriety (or Save Our Selves), National Clearinghouse, P.O. Box 5, Buffalo, NY 14215-0005; (716) 834-2922. A non-higher-power-oriented alternative to Alcoholics Anonymous.

Sexaholics Anonymous, P.O. Box 300, Simi Valley, CA 93602.

The Silent Passage: Menopause, by Gail Sheehy (Random House, 1992). An attempt to erase the "stigma of menopause" by bringing it into the open; includes social and medical information.

Staying Power: Long Term Lesbian Couples, by Susan E. Johnson (Naiad, 1990). Based on a study of 108 couples; includes statistics and extensive quotes.

Unbroken Ties: Lesbian Ex-Lovers, by Carol S. Becker (Alyson, 1988). A guide to surviving a breakup and dealing with your ex.

Violent Betrayal: Partner Abuse in Lesbian Relationships, by Claire M. Renzetti (Sage, 1992). An examination of battering in lesbian relationships from a sociological point of view. Tends toward statistics, but also includes case studies.

SEX

Coming to Power: Writings and Graphics on Lesbian S/M, edited by members of SAMOIS (Alyson Publications, 1982). Includes S/M fiction, theory, and safety tips.

Discover magazine (June 1992). An entire issue on sex, including articles on bonobos, the evolution of the orgasm, and why we know so little about human sexuality.

For Yourself: The Fulfillment of Female Sexuality, by Lonnie Garfield Barbach (New American Library, 1975). Gets low points for its treatment of lesbianism (reassures straight women that fantasizing about women won't make them gay), but does provide excellent information about achieving or improving orgasms.

The Gay Report, by Karla Jay and Allen Young (Summit Books, 1977). Out of date, out of print, and hard to find; detailed statistical examination of the sexual habits of lesbians and gay men.

The G Spot and Other Recent Discoveries about Human Sexuality, by Alice Kahn Ladas, Beverly Whipple, and John D. Perry (Holt, Rinehart & Winston, 1982). The book that made the G-spot famous.

The Hite Report, by Shere Hite (Macmillan, 1976). About women and sexuality; filled with quotes and statistics.

Homosexualities: A Study of Diversity among Men and Women, by Alan P. Bell and Martin S. Weinberg (Simon & Schuster, 1978). A highly statistical analysis of the sexual habits of lesbians and gay men as of the 1970s.

How to Female Ejaculate, Fatale Video, 526 Castro Street, San Francisco, CA 94114; (800) 845-4617. A how-to video about G-spot orgasms and ejaculation; includes footage of women coming.

The Joy of Lesbian Sex, by Dr. Emily L. Sisley and Bertha Harris (Crown Publishers, 1977). Out of print and out of date; interesting as a historical document.

The Lesbian Erotic Dance: Butch, Femme, Androgyny and Other Rhythms, by JoAnn Loulan (Spinsters Book Company, 1990). An exploration of the various ways lesbians relate to one another sexually, with extensive quotes and information from surveys.

Lesbian Passion: Loving Ourselves and Each Other, by JoAnn Loulan (Spinsters/Aunt Lute, 1987). Explores the role of passion, sexual and otherwise, in lesbians' lives. With an emphasis on the role of recovery in sexuality.

Lesbian Sex, by JoAnn Loulan (Spinsters Ink, 1984). For women recovering from sexism, homophobia, and various types of abuse. Includes extensive exercises for expanding the capacity to enjoy and participate in sex.

The Lesbian S/M Safety Manual, edited by Pat Califia (Lace Publications, 1988). A must-read for anyone interested in S/M.

On Our Backs, 526 Castro Street, San Francisco, CA 94114; (800) 845-4617. Self-described as "entertainment for the adventurous lesbian," this magazine includes fiction, opinion, advice, photographs, and how-to info, with a definite, but not exclusive, leaning toward S/M.

Sapphistry: The Book of Lesbian Sexuality, by Pat Califia, illustrated by Tee Corinne (Naiad Press, 1988). A general guide to lesbian sex.

Sex for One: The Joy of Selfloving, by Betty Dodson (Harmony Books, 1987). Explores the joys of masturbation for gay and straight women and men.

Sexual Behavior in the Human Female, by the staff of the Institute for Sex Research, Indiana University (Alfred C. Kinsey et al.; W.B. Saunders, 1953). For many years considered the ultimate authority on female sexuality; still offers insights to anyone interested in sex.

Susie Sexpert's Lesbian Sex World, by Susie Bright (Cleis Press, 1990). A collection of columns from *On Our Backs* for the dyke who wants to boldly go where she might not have gone before. Combines nuts-and-bolts info with infectious enthusiasm.

Susie Bright's Sexual Reality: A Virtual Sex World Reader (Cleis Press, 1992). More essays on sex; includes "Shiny Plastic Dildos Holding Hands," "Story of O Birthday Party," and "I Got This Way from Kissing Donahue."

**alyson
books**

AFTERGLOW, *edited by Karen Barber.* Filled with the excitement of new love and the remembrances of past ones, *Afterglow* offers well-crafted, imaginative, sexy stories of lesbian desire.

DREAM LOVER, *by Jane Futcher.* The enduring power of adolescent fantasy tempts one woman at an emotional crossroads in later life.

EARLY EMBRACES, *by Lindsey Elder.* Sexily sizzling or softly sensual stories explore the first lesbian experience for women.

THE FEMME MYSTIQUE, *edited by Lesléa Newman. Women's Monthly* says, "Images of so-called 'lipstick lesbians' have become the darlings of the popular media of late. *The Femme Mystique* brings together a broad range of work in which 'real' lesbians who self-identify as femmes speak for themselves about what it means to be femme today."

HEATWAVE: WOMEN IN LOVE AND LUST, *edited by Lucy Jane Bledsoe.* Where can a woman go when she needs a good hot…read? Crawl between the covers of *Heatwave,* a collection of original short stories about women in search of that elusive thing called love.

THE LESBIAN SEX BOOK, *by Wendy Caster.* Informative, entertaining, and attractively illustrated, this handbook is the lesbian sex guide for the '90s. Dealing with lesbian sex practices in a practical, nonjudgmental way, this guide is perfect for the newly out and the eternally curious.

THE PERSISTENT DESIRE, *edited by Joan Nestle.* A generation ago butch-femme identities were taken for granted in the lesbian community. Today, women who think of themselves as butch or femme often face prejudice from both the lesbian community and the straight world. Here, for the first time, dozens of femme and butch lesbians tell their stories of love, survival, and triumph.

PILLOW TALK, *edited by Lesléa Newman.* Climb into bed with this collection of well-crafted, imaginative, and sexy stories: an unbridled celebration of lesbian eroticism. These tales simmer with intrigue, lusty encounters, and lots of hot sex between the sheets as well as some other creative places. These spicy stories will leave you begging for more!